The Ultimate Mediterranean Diet Cookbook for Beginners:

2000+ Days of Super Easy 30-Minute Recipes with a 30-Day Meal Plan & Shopping List to Improve Your Well-Being and Maintain a Healthy Weight.

Thomas O. Harvey

Copyright © 2025 by .Thomas O.Harvey All rights reserved.

No portion of this book may be reproduced, transmitted, or distributed in any form or by any method without prior written consent from the publisher, except for brief quotations used in reviews or critical articles.

Legal & Disclaimer

The material and information provided in this book have been gathered from reliable sources and are presented with the best knowledge, belief, and expertise of the author. However, the author assumes no responsibility for any omissions or errors.

TABLE OF CONTENTS

INTRODUCTION 6
CHAPTER 1: 30-DAY MEAL PLAN 10
CHAPTER 2: Smart Grocery Planning 12
    Grocery Shopping List for 7-Day Meal Plan .. 12
    Grocery Shopping List for 8-14 Day Meal Plan 13
    Grocery Shopping List for 15-21 Day Meal Plan 14
    Grocery Shopping List for 22-30 Day Meal Plan 15

CHAPTER 3: BREAKFAST: Warm & Wholesome Mornings 17
    QUINOA BREAKFAST BOWL WITH BERRIES AND ALMONDS 17
    CAULIFLOWER SCRAMBLE WITH FETA AND OREGANO 17
    WARM APPLE-CINNAMON MILLET WITH WALNUTS 18
    MEDITERRANEAN EGG SKILLET WITH TOMATO & GREENS 18
    CARROT-OAT PANCAKES WITH YOGURT DRIZZLE 19
    RED LENTIL PORRIDGE WITH OLIVE OIL AND HERBS 19

CHAPTER 4: BREAKFAST: Light Yet Satisfying 20
    GREEK YOGURT BOWL WITH ORANGE SEGMENTS AND PISTACHIOS 20
    BUCKWHEAT WITH STEWED PLUMS AND SUNFLOWER SEEDS 20
    BAKED RICOTTA WITH ROASTED STRAWBERRIES 21
    MUSHROOM-EGG STIR WITH THYME AND BABY SPINACH 21
    PUMPKIN PUREE PORRIDGE WITH CINNAMON AND CHIA 22
    OATMEAL WITH PEAR, FLAXSEED, AND CRUSHED ALMONDS 22
    COTTAGE CHEESE WITH STEAMED APPLES AND POPPY SEEDS 23
    VEGETABLE MEDLEY BAKE WITH EGG AND BASIL 23
    CHAPTER 5: BREAKFAST: Comfort Bowls 24
    MILLET PORRIDGE WITH DRIED APRICOTS AND ALMOND BUTTER 24
    SCRAMBLED EGGS WITH SAUTÉED KALE AND RED ONION 24
    RICE & CHICKPEA BOWL WITH OLIVE TAPENADE CRUMBLE 25
    ZUCCHINI-CARROT PANCAKES WITH YOGURT-HERB DIP 25
    APPLE-WALNUT FARRO WITH GREEK YOGURT CREAM 26
    MASHED SWEET POTATO WITH POACHED EGG AND DILL 26
    OATS WITH BAKED PEACH AND PUMPKIN SEEDS 27
    SPINACH-TOMATO EGG MUFFINS (BAKED STYLE) 27

CHAPTER 6: BREAKFAST: Savory Balance 28
    LENTIL & TOMATO STEW WITH SOFT-BOILED EGG 28
    EGGPLANT & BELL PEPPER RAGOUT WITH HERBS 28
    CHICKPEA & LEEK MASH WITH CUMIN AND PARSLEY 29
    BARLEY BREAKFAST RISOTTO WITH ZUCCHINI AND EGG 29
    WARM RICOTTA & FIG BOWL WITH CRUSHED HAZELNUTS 30
    STEAMED BROCCOLI WITH EGG AND YOGURT DRESSING 30
    CAULIFLOWER MASH WITH POACHED EGG AND OLIVE OIL 31
    ROASTED PUMPKIN WITH FETA AND FRESH THYME 31

CHAPTER 7: LUNCH: Earthy & Nourishing Bowls 32
    CHICKPEA & SPINACH STEW WITH ROASTED GARLIC 32
    GRILLED CHICKEN WITH BULGUR AND LEMON-ZUCCHINI 32
    RED LENTIL CURRY WITH CARROT AND BROWN RICE 33
    BAKED COD WITH SWEET POTATO AND OLIVE RELISH 33
    QUINOA BOWL WITH ROASTED VEGETABLES AND FETA 34
    TURKEY MEATBALLS WITH

TOMATO-BARLEY RAGU............................ 34

BROCCOLI & CAULIFLOWER STIR WITH TAHINI-LIME SAUCE............................ 35

WILD RICE WITH MUSHROOMS AND POACHED EGG............................ 35

CHAPTER 8: LUNCH: Hearty Mediterranean Plates............................ 36

RATATOUILLE WITH WHITE BEANS AND HERBS DE PROVENCE............................ 36

LEMON-HERB CHICKEN THIGHS WITH COUSCOUS............................ 36

ZUCCHINI BOATS STUFFED WITH GROUND TURKEY & FARRO............................ 37

ROASTED BELL PEPPER & CHICKPEA BOWL WITH CUMIN YOGURT............................ 37

COD FILLET WITH GREEN BEANS AND GARLIC-MASHED POTATO............................ 38

LENTIL STEW WITH CARROTS, CELERY, AND OLIVE OIL DRIZZLE............................ 38

EGGPLANT & TOMATO BAKE WITH BASIL RICOTTA............................ 39

GRILLED SHRIMP WITH BULGUR-PARSLEY SALAD............................ 39

CHAPTER 9: LUNCH: Plant-Based Comforts... 40

CANNELLINI BEAN STEW WITH SPINACH AND TOMATOES............................ 40

WARM FARRO & VEGETABLE BOWL WITH POACHED EGG............................ 40

ROASTED PUMPKIN WITH LENTILS AND SPICED YOGURT............................ 41

BAKED FALAFEL BOWL WITH QUINOA AND LEMON-HERB SAUCE............................ 41

STUFFED TOMATOES WITH BROWN RICE AND HERBS............................ 42

CAULIFLOWER & PEA CURRY WITH WHOLE GRAIN RICE............................ 42

CHICKPEA PATTIES WITH CARROT SLAW AND YOGURT DIP............................ 43

POLENTA WITH SAUTÉED KALE AND WHITE BEANS............................ 43

CHAPTER 10: LUNCH: Balanced Protein Mains............................ 44

GRILLED SALMON WITH BROCCOLI AND LEMON COUSCOUS............................ 44

TURKEY & CHICKPEA BOWL WITH OLIVE DRESSING............................ 44

BAKED WHITE FISH WITH LENTILS AND TOMATO SALSA............................ 45

CHICKEN & EGGPLANT SAUTÉ WITH COUSCOUS............................ 4

SPAGHETTI SQUASH WITH SARDINES AND CAPERS............................ 4

ZUCCHINI-LENTIL CAKES WITH GARLIC YOGURT............................ 4

SHRIMP & BELL PEPPER STIR-FRY WITH BARLEY (WITH OLIVE OIL BOOST)............................ 4

SAUTÉED MUSHROOMS AND BEANS WITH POACHED EGG............................ 4

CHAPTER 11: SNACK: With a spoon and with pleasure............................ 4

RICOTTA CREAM WITH STEWED PEACHES AND CINNAMON............................ 4

CHIA PUDDING WITH BAKED BERRIES AND VANILLA............................ 4

COTTAGE CHEESE MOUSSE WITH GRATED APPLE AND NUTMEG............................ 4

YOGURT & PUMPKIN PURÉE WITH CLOVE AND ORANGE ZEST............................ 4

PEAR COMPOTE WITH YOGURT AND SESAME CRUMBLE............................ 5

MASHED BANANA CUSTARD WITH LEMON AND CARDAMOM............................ 5

WARM QUINOA DESSERT WITH DATE SYRUP AND COCONUT MILK............................ 5

CREAMY CARROT PUDDING WITH RAISINS AND CINNAMON............................ 5

CHAPTER 12: SNACK: Baked Delights............ 5

HONEY-RICOTTA APPLE BOATS WITH TOASTED ALMOND DUST............................ 5

BALSAMIC-GLAZED FIGS WITH CREAMY YOGURT CLOUDS............................ 5

VELVETY PUMPKIN YOGURT BOWL WITH POMEGRANATE JEWELS............................ 5

WARM PEAR DELIGHT WITH VANILLA-SCENTED COTTAGE CREAM. 5

ZUCCHINI CITRUS CUSTARD WITH ORANGE ZEST AND OLIVE OIL CRUMBS 54

CINNAMON-STEAM BANANA CAKE WITH DATE SYRUP DRIZZLE............................ 5

ROASTED PLUM PARCELS WITH LEMON-RICOTTA HEART............................ 5

CARAMELIZED PEACH HALVES WITH SESAME YOGURT SWIRL............................ 5

CHAPTER 13: Light Creams and Mousses........ 5

DATE-BANANA MOUSSE WITH YOGURT

AND COCOA..56
LIGHT FIG CREAM WITH RICOTTA AND MINT..56
ORANGE-RAISIN SEMOLINA WITH GREEK YOGURT..57
LENTIL-DATE DESSERT PURÉE WITH ROSE WATER..57
APPLE-CINNAMON MILLET CREAM WITH YOGURT..58
GRAPE COMPOTE WITH RICOTTA AND LEMON ZEST..58

CHAPTER 14: SNACK: Satisfying Mediterranean..59

SPICED LENTIL-APPLE BITES WITH YOGURT DIP..59
MINI STUFFED PEPPERS WITH HERBED FETA AND OLIVES..59
ROASTED GRAPES WITH GOAT CHEESE AND WALNUTS..60
CUCUMBER BOATS WITH TUNA, CAPERS & SUN-DRIED TOMATO..60
WARM DATE-ALMOND COUSCOUS CUPS..61
EGGPLANT CHIPS WITH TOMATO-FETA SALSA..61

CHAPTER 15: DINNER: Vegetable-Focused & Light..62

SWEET POTATO & SPINACH STEW WITH PAPRIKA OIL..62
WHITE BEAN & SWISS CHARD SAUTÉ WITH LEMON AND OLIVE OIL..62
BRAISED EGGPLANT WITH TOMATOES AND GARLIC..63
STUFFED ZUCCHINI WITH HERBED BULGUR AND TOMATOES..63
CAULIFLOWER BAKE WITH TOMATO, FETA, AND OREGANO..64
CHICKPEA TAGINE WITH ROASTED CARROTS AND MINT..64
GRILLED VEGETABLES WITH LABNEH AND WALNUTS..65
POLENTA WITH ROASTED CHERRY TOMATOES AND THYME..65

CHAPTER 16: DINNER: Seafood & Satisfaction..66

GRILLED SARDINES WITH LEMON AND PARSLEY OVER GREENS..66
BAKED COD WITH GARLIC CHICKPEAS AND SPINACH..66
SHRIMP & TOMATO SKILLET WITH CAPERS AND ZUCCHINI..67
TROUT FILLET WITH COUSCOUS AND ROASTED PEPPERS..67
MACKEREL WITH WARM LENTIL SALAD AND RED ONION..68
SEAFOOD & FENNEL SOUP WITH OLIVE DRIZZLE..68

CHAPTER 17: DINNER: Light Poultry Dishes.. 69

BRAISED CHICKEN THIGH WITH OLIVES AND TOMATOES..69
HERBED TURKEY MEATBALLS WITH SPINACH BULGUR PILAF..69
CHICKEN WITH ROASTED EGGPLANT AND GARLIC YOGURT..70
LEMON CHICKEN SKILLET WITH ZUCCHINI AND PEPPERS..70
STUFFED PEPPERS WITH GROUND TURKEY AND COUSCOUS..71
POACHED CHICKEN WITH LENTILS AND LEMON-PARSLEY OIL..71
GRILLED CHICKEN WITH TOMATO, OLIVE, AND ARUGULA SALAD..72
WARM CHICKPEA-CHICKEN BOWL WITH MINT YOGURT..72

CHAPTER 18: DINNER: Grain & Plant Harmony..73

FARRO SALAD WITH ROASTED VEGETABLES AND FETA..73
WARM LENTILS WITH CARROTS, LEEKS, AND TAHINI DRIZZLE..73
BARLEY PILAF WITH MUSHROOMS AND CUMIN YOGURT..74
QUINOA BOWL WITH ZUCCHINI, CHICKPEAS, AND LEMON OIL..74
BROWN RICE WITH TOMATO, SPINACH, AND PINE NUTS..75
MILLET WITH ROASTED CAULIFLOWER AND RAISINS..75
COUSCOUS WITH ROASTED SQUASH, CHICKPEAS, AND HERBS..76
WILD RICE & ROASTED EGGPLANT WITH GARLIC SAUCE..76

INTRODUCTION

Welcome to a Better Way of Eating — and Living

If you've ever felt overwhelmed by dieting rules, calorie tracking apps, or exhausting "health hacks," you're not alone. In a world of extremes and quick fixes, the Mediterranean way offers something radically different — balance, joy, and real food that nourishes both your body and spirit.

This cookbook was created for people just like you — busy individuals who want to eat well, feel energized, and build habits that actually last. Whether your goal is to improve your well-being, manage your weight, or simply cook meals that taste incredible without spending hours in the kitchen, you're in the right place.

What Makes This Book Different?

- 2000+ Days of recipes designed for real life — fast, easy, flavorful
- A complete 30-Day Meal Plan to remove the guesswork
- Weekly shopping lists to simplify prep
- Nutrient-rich dishes built around Mediterranean staples: fresh vegetables, whole grains, lean proteins, healthy fats, and vibrant herbs

This is more than a collection of recipes — it's an invitation to return to the basics of good living. To slow down. To reconnect with your food. To rediscover the simple pleasure of preparing a meal that fuels your energy and supports your health.

No complicated ingredients. No restrictive rules. Just one delicious, heart-healthy step at a time.

Let's begin your Mediterranean journey — the easy, delicious, and sustainable way.

What Is the Mediterranean Diet?

A Lifestyle Rooted in Centuries of Wisdom

The Mediterranean Diet isn't a fad or a quick fix — it's a time-tested way of living and eating that's been cherished for generations in countries like Greece, Italy, Spain, and along the coasts of the Middle East and North Africa. These regions are known not only for their flavorful food, but also for the health, longevity, and vitality of the people who live there.

At its core, the Mediterranean Diet is based on fresh, whole foods, prepared simply and shared with others. It celebrates abundance — not restriction — and centers around meals that are colorful, satisfying, and deeply nourishing.

But what exactly does "Mediterranean" mean on your plate?

It means more:

- More vegetables, legumes, whole grains, nuts, seeds, and fruits
- More olive oil and healthy fats
- More seafood and lean poultry
- More herbs, garlic, lemon, and natural flavor

nd less:

- Less red meat, sugar, and processed foods
- Less refined oils and artificial ingredients
- Less stress around perfection — and more joy around eating

cientifically Backed — Naturally elicious

ountless studies have shown that the editerranean Diet can:

- Lower the risk of heart disease, stroke, and type 2 diabetes
- Improve brain function and reduce inflammation
- Support healthy weight management
- Promote longer life and higher quality of life

ut beyond the science, here's what truly ets it apart: it's not a diet you start and stop. s a sustainable rhythm of living — flexible, rgiving, and full of flavor.

hether you're cooking for yourself, a artner, or a whole family, the Mediterranean pproach adapts to your needs. It doesn't sk for perfection — only intention.

he Core Principles of the Mediterranean ifestyle

imple Guidelines for Lifelong Well-Being

ne Mediterranean lifestyle isn't about rules - it's about rhythms. It's about making daily noices that nourish your body, support your ealth, and bring pleasure to your table.

ere's how to bring the Mediterranean pproach into your life — one delicious day a time.

● 1. Eat More Plants

Focus on seasonal vegetables, leafy greens, beans, lentils, and fruits. These form the foundation of nearly every Mediterranean meal. Think: colorful salads, hearty stews, roasted vegetables, and fruit as a natural dessert.

2. Choose Whole Grains

Swap refined carbs for fiber-rich grains like farro, bulgur, brown rice, barley, and whole-grain bread. These keep you full longer, stabilize blood sugar, and pair beautifully with herbs and olive oil.

3. Favor Fish & Lean Protein

Eat more seafood, especially oily fish like salmon, sardines, and mackerel — rich in omega-3s. Enjoy poultry in moderation, and keep red meat occasional.

● 4. Use Olive Oil Generously

Make extra virgin olive oil your go-to fat for cooking, dressing, and drizzling. It's loaded with heart-healthy antioxidants and adds richness to every dish.

5. Enjoy Dairy in Moderation

Greek yogurt, feta, and aged cheeses are part of the Mediterranean table — just in smaller portions. Use them to complement meals, not dominate them.

6. Snack Smart

Nuts, seeds, olives, and fresh fruits make for energizing, wholesome snacks. Say goodbye to processed chips and candy — and hello to crunch with purpose.

7. Flavor with Herbs, Not Salt

Enhance meals with basil, oregano, parsley, thyme, garlic, lemon juice, and vinegar. These bring bold, natural flavor — without relying on sodium or heavy sauces.

8. Eat Mindfully and Socially

Take time to savor your food. Share meals with family or friends. Enjoy real conversations around the table. These rituals are as important as the food itself.

9. Stay Active, Naturally

The Mediterranean lifestyle isn't about intense workouts — it's about movement built into your day. Walking, gardening, dancing, taking the stairs — it all counts.

10. Live with Joy and Balance

It's not about perfection — it's about consistency. Treats are welcome. Wine is optional. Self-care and sleep are essential. This is a lifestyle you can love — and live with.

Health Benefits of the Mediterranean Diet

Backed by Science. Proven in Real Life.

You don't need to overhaul your entire life to feel better — just start with your plate.
The Mediterranean Diet has been studied more than any other way of eating, and the verdict is clear: this lifestyle isn't just delicious — it's one of the healthiest in the world.

1. Protects Your Heart

A diet rich in olive oil, vegetables, and fish helps reduce inflammation, improve cholesterol, and lower blood pressure — three major risk factors for heart disease. In fact, the Mediterranean Diet has been shown to reduce the risk of heart attacks and strokes by up to 30%.

2. Boosts Brain Function

Numerous studies link this diet to better memory, sharper focus, and a lower risk of Alzheimer's and cognitive decline. Antioxidants from fruits, vegetables, and olive oil may protect the brain from aging.

3. Supports Healthy Weight Loss

Forget strict calorie counting. The Mediterranean Diet helps you feel full and satisfied thanks to healthy fats, fiber, and whole foods — naturally reducing cravings and overeating without restriction or stress.

4. Fights Inflammation

Chronic inflammation is linked to many conditions, from joint pain to autoimmune disease. Mediterranean staples like leafy greens, omega-3-rich fish, and nuts help cool inflammation from the inside out.

5. Improves Gut Health

Fermented dairy, legumes, fiber-rich grains, and vegetables feed your gut's good bacteria — which play a critical role in digestion, mood, immunity, and metabolism.

6. Reduces Risk of Chronic Illness

This diet has been shown to help manage or prevent conditions like:

- Type 2 diabetes
- High blood pressure
- Obesity
- Certain cancers
- Depression

And it does all of this *without deprivation* — just real food, prepared simply and enjoyed regularly.

🌿 Real Results, Real Life

You don't have to be perfect to feel the benefits. Even small shifts — like cooking with olive oil instead of butter or adding a side of greens to your plate — can move you in the right direction.

This is why the Mediterranean Diet works: it's flexible, forgiving, and designed for everyday people with real lives.

How to Use This Book Effectively

Your Roadmap to Simpler Meals, Smarter Planning, and Lasting Change

This book was designed to take the stress out of healthy eating. Whether you're flipping through recipes on a weeknight or following the full 30-day plan, everything here is structured to make your journey smooth, flexible, and enjoyable.

Here's how to get the most out of it:

■ 1. Start with the 30-Day Meal Plan

You'll find a complete 30-day Mediterranean meal plan — carefully balanced with unique breakfasts, lunches, snacks, and dinners for every single day.

- No repeated meals
- All recipes take 30 minutes or less
- Nutritionally balanced with real ingredients
- Designed for energy, weight balance, and satisfaction

If you're new to the Mediterranean lifestyle, the meal plan is your shortcut to getting started — no guesswork required.

🛒 2. Use the Weekly Grocery Lists

Each week of the meal plan comes with a detailed shopping list — organized by category (produce, dairy, pantry, etc.) to make your grocery trip fast and efficient.

■ No more wandering the store
■ No forgotten ingredients
■ No wasted food

Want to batch cook or prep ahead? The lists are flexible and great for meal prep, too.

CHAPTER 1: 30-DAY MEAL PLAN

Table 1: Days 1–15

Day	Breakfast	Lunch	Snack	Dinner
Day 1	Zucchini-Carrot Pancakes with Yogurt-Herb Dip – p.25	Cannellini Bean Stew with Spinach and Tomatoes – p.40	Chia Pudding with Baked Berries and Vanilla – p.48	Braised Chicken Thigh with Olives and Tomatoes – p.69
Day 2	Cottage Cheese with Steamed Apples and Poppy Seeds – p.23	Grilled Salmon with Broccoli and Lemon Couscous – p.44	Eggplant Chips with Tomato-Feta Salsa – p.61	Warm Lentils with Carrots, Leeks, and Tahini Drizzle – p.73
Day 3	Baked Ricotta with Roasted Strawberries – p.21	Chickpea & Spinach Stew with Roasted Garlic – p.32	Warm Pear Delight with Vanilla-Scented Cottage Cream – p.53	Grilled Vegetables with Labneh and Walnuts – p.65
Day 4	Warm Apple-Cinnamon Millet with Walnuts – p.18	Shrimp & Bell Pepper Stir-Fry with Barley – p.47	Date-Banana Mousse with Yogurt and Cocoa – p.56	Couscous with Roasted Squash, Chickpeas, and Herbs – p.76
Day 5	Red Lentil Porridge with Olive Oil and Herbs – p.19	Quinoa Bowl with Roasted Vegetables and Feta – p.34	Ricotta Cream with Stewed Peaches and Cinnamon – p.48	Shrimp & Tomato Skillet with Capers and Zucchini – p.67
Day 6	Buckwheat with Stewed Plums and Sunflower Seeds – p.20	Eggplant & Tomato Bake with Basil Ricotta – p.39	Lentil-Date Dessert Purée with Rose Water – p.57	Farro Salad with Roasted Vegetables and Feta – p.73
Day 7	Spinach-Tomato Egg Muffins (Baked Style) – p.27	Turkey Meatballs with Tomato-Barley Ragu – p.34	Caramelized Peach Halves with Sesame Yogurt Swirl – p.55	Poached Chicken with Lentils and Lemon-Parsley Oil – p.71
Day 8	Barley Breakfast Risotto with Zucchini and Egg – p.29	Chicken & Eggplant Sauté with Couscous – p.45	Grape Compote with Ricotta and Lemon Zest – p.58	Baked Cod with Garlic Chickpeas and Spinach – p.66
Day 9	Apple-Walnut Farro with Greek Yogurt Cream – p.26	Lentil Stew with Carrots, Celery, and Olive Oil Drizzle – p.38	Cinnamon-Steam Banana Cake with Date Syrup Drizzle – p.54	Sweet Potato & Spinach Stew with Paprika Oil – p.62
Day 10	Steamed Broccoli with Egg and Yogurt Dressing – p.30	Stuffed Tomatoes with Brown Rice and Herbs – p.42	Balsamic-Glazed Figs with Creamy Yogurt Clouds – p.52	Mackerel with Warm Lentil Salad and Red Onion – p.68
Day 11	Scrambled Eggs with Sautéed Kale and Red Onion – p.24	Zucchini Boats Stuffed with Ground Turkey & Farro – p.37	Spiced Lentil-Apple Bites with Yogurt Dip – p.59	Wild Rice & Roasted Eggplant with Garlic Sauce – p.76
Day 12	Cauliflower Scramble with Feta and Oregano – p.17	Ratatouille with White Beans and Herbes de Provence – p.36	Warm Quinoa Dessert with Date Syrup and Coconut Milk – p.51	Grilled Chicken with Tomato, Olive, and Arugula Salad – p.72
Day 13	Pumpkin Purée Porridge with Cinnamon and Chia – p.22	Roasted Bell Pepper & Chickpea Bowl with Cumin Yogurt – p.37	Orange-Raisin Semolina with Greek Yogurt – p.57	White Bean & Swiss Chard Sauté with Lemon and Olive Oil – p.62
Day 14	Mashed Sweet Potato with Poached Egg and Dill – p.26	Warm Farro & Vegetable Bowl with Poached Egg – p.40	Yogurt & Pumpkin Purée with Clove and Orange Zest – p.49	Herbed Turkey Meatballs with Spinach Bulgur Pilaf – p.69
Day 15	Mushroom-Egg Stir with Thyme and Baby Spinach – p.21	Turkey & Chickpea Bowl with Olive Dressing – p.44	Roasted Grapes with Goat Cheese and Walnuts – p.60	Baked Falafel Bowl with Quinoa and Lemon-Herb Sauce – p.41

Table 2: Days 16–30

Day	Breakfast	Lunch	Snack	Dinner
Day 16	Chickpea & Leek Mash with Cumin and Parsley – p.29	Cod Fillet with Green Beans and Garlic-Mashed Potato – p.38	Cottage Cheese Mousse with Grated Apple and Nutmeg – p.49	Grilled Sardines with Lemon and Parsley over Greens – p.66
Day 17	Greek Yogurt Bowl with Orange Segments and Pistachios – p.20	Polenta with Sautéed Kale and White Beans – p.43	Mini Stuffed Peppers with Herbed Feta and Olives – p.59	Chicken with Roasted Eggplant and Garlic Yogurt – p.70
Day 18	Vegetable Medley Bake with Egg and Basil – p.23	Red Lentil Curry with Carrot and Brown Rice – p.33	Apple-Cinnamon Millet Cream with Yogurt – p.58	Trout Fillet with Couscous and Roasted Peppers – p.67
Day 19	Cauliflower Mash with Poached Egg and Olive Oil – p.31	Chickpea Patties with Carrot Slaw and Yogurt Dip – p.43	Roasted Plum Parcels with Lemon-Ricotta Heart – p.55	Barley Pilaf with Mushrooms and Cumin Yogurt – p.74
Day 20	Warm Ricotta & Fig Bowl with Crushed Hazelnuts – p.30	Grilled Shrimp with Bulgur-Parsley Salad – p.39	Pear Compote with Yogurt and Sesame Crumble – p.50	Stuffed Zucchini with Herbed Bulgur and Tomatoes – p.63
Day 21	Quinoa Breakfast Bowl with Berries and Almonds – p.17	Lemon-Herb Chicken Thighs with Couscous – p.36	Velvety Pumpkin Yogurt Bowl with Pomegranate Jewels – p.53	Chickpea Tagine with Roasted Carrots and Mint – p.64
Day 22	Lentil & Tomato Stew with Soft-Boiled Egg – p.28	Cauliflower & Pea Curry with Whole Grain Rice – p.42	Zucchini Citrus Custard with Orange Zest and Olive Oil Crumbs – p.54	Grilled Chicken with Tomato, Olive, and Arugula Salad – p.72
Day 23	Millet Porridge with Dried Apricots and Almond Butter – p.24	Baked Cod with Sweet Potato and Olive Relish – p.33	Spiced Lentil-Apple Bites with Yogurt Dip – p.59	Wild Rice with Roasted Eggplant and Garlic Sauce – p.76
Day 24	Zucchini-Carrot Pancakes with Yogurt-Herb Dip – p.25	Spaghetti Squash with Sardines and Capers – p.46	Light Fig Cream with Ricotta and Mint – p.56	Braised Eggplant with Tomatoes and Garlic – p.63
Day 25	Oatmeal with Pear, Flaxseed, and Crushed Almonds – p.22	Stuffed Peppers with Ground Turkey and Couscous – p.71	Warm Date-Almond Couscous Cups – p.61	Seafood & Fennel Soup with Olive Drizzle – p.68
Day 26	Rice & Chickpea Bowl with Olive Tapenade Crumble – p.25	Warm Lentils with Carrots, Leeks, and Tahini Drizzle – p.73	Honey-Ricotta Apple Boats with Toasted Almond Dust – p.52	White Bean & Swiss Chard Sauté with Lemon and Olive Oil – p.62
Day 27	Eggplant & Bell Pepper Ragout with Herbs – p.28	Turkey & Chickpea Bowl with Olive Dressing – p.44	Mashed Banana Custard with Lemon and Cardamom – p.50	Lemon Chicken Skillet with Zucchini and Peppers – p.70
Day 28	Carrot-Oat Pancakes with Yogurt Drizzle – p.19	Baked White Fish with Lentils and Tomato Salsa – p.45	Orange-Raisin Semolina with Greek Yogurt – p.57	Quinoa Bowl with Zucchini, Chickpeas, and Lemon Oil – p.74
Day 29	Savory Mediterranean Egg Skillet with Tomato & Greens – p.18	Roasted Pumpkin with Lentils and Spiced Yogurt – p.41	Cucumber Boats with Tuna, Capers & Sun-Dried Tomato – p.60	Grilled Vegetables with Labneh and Walnuts – p.65
Day 30	Oats with Baked Peach and Pumpkin Seeds – p.27	Cannellini Bean Stew with Spinach and Tomatoes – p.40	Grape Compote with Ricotta and Lemon Zest – p.58	Brown Rice with Tomato, Spinach, and Pine Nuts – p.75

CHAPTER 2: Smart Grocery Planning

Staying committed to a heart-healthy Mediterranean lifestyle doesn't happen by chance — it begins with thoughtful planning and the right tools to support your journey. That's why this book includes a complete 30-day meal plan alongside meticulously crafted grocery shopping lists, designed to simplify your routine, keep your kitchen organized, and make healthy choices effortless.

Each 7-day shopping list is seamlessly connected to the recipes in your meal plan, showing you exactly what to buy, how much to prepare, and how to stay on track — without the stress of last-minute decisions or wasted food.

Grocery Shopping List for 7-Day Meal Plan

Vegetables
Zucchini – 2 medium (Zucchini-Carrot Pancakes, Shrimp Stir-Fry)
Carrot – 3 medium (Zucchini-Carrot Pancakes, Lentil Curry)
Cauliflower – 1 small head (Cauliflower Scramble, Cauliflower-Tahini Stir)
Spinach – 6 cups / 180g (Spinach-Tomato Muffins, Bean Stew, Chicken Bowl)
Broccoli – 1 small head (Grilled Salmon, Shrimp Stir-Fry)
Bell peppers – 3 (Egg Muffins, Shrimp Stir-Fry, Chicken Bowl)
Tomatoes – 4 medium (Mediterranean Egg Skillet, Eggplant Bake)
Cherry tomatoes – 1 cup / 150g (Farro Salad)
Red onion – 2 small (Scrambled Eggs, Farro Salad)
Yellow onion – 2 medium (Lentil Curry, Turkey Ragu)
Garlic – 1 bulb (Spinach Stew, Ragu, Eggplant Bake)
Sweet potato – 2 small (Baked Cod, Apple-Farro Bowl)
Mushrooms – 1 cup / 100g (Mushroom Stir, Wild Rice Bowl)
Eggplant – 2 small (Eggplant Bake, Chicken-Eggplant Dish)
Green beans – 1 cup / 120g (Cod Fillet with Garlic Mash)
Leeks – 1 stalk (Leek Mash)
Celery – 1 stalk (Lentil Stew)
Kale – 1 cup chopped / 30g (Scrambled Eggs, Sausage-Kale Bowl)

Fruits
Apples – 2 (Steamed Apple Cottage Cheese, Apple-Farro Bowl)
Plums – 2 (Buckwheat with Stewed Plums)
Berries (mixed) – 1/2 cup / 75g (Quinoa Breakfast Bowl)
Peach – 1 (Oats with Baked Peach)
Lemon – 3 (Salmon, Chicken Bowl, Farro Salad)
Orange – 1 (Greek Yogurt Bowl)
Banana – 1 (Date-Banana Mousse)
Dates (pitted) – 6 (Mousse, Quinoa Dessert)
Fig (fresh or dried) – 2 (Ricotta-Fig Bowl)
Grapes – 1/2 cup / 75g (Grape Compote)
Strawberries – 1/2 cup / 75g (Baked Ricotta)

Grains & Legumes
Quinoa – 1/2 cup dry / 90g (Quinoa Bowl, Falafel Bowl)
Brown rice – 1/2 cup dry / 90g (Lentil Curry)
Bulgur – 1/2 cup dry / 90g (Grilled Chicken with Bulgur)
Whole barley – 1/4 cup dry / 50g (Breakfast Risotto)
Wild rice – 1/4 cup dry / 50g (Wild Rice with Mushrooms)
Farro – 1/3 cup dry / 60g (Apple-Farro Bowl, Farro Salad)
Rolled oats – 3/4 cup / 70g (Oats with Baked Peach, Carrot-Oat Pancakes)
Millet – 1/4 cup dry / 50g (Warm Millet with Walnuts)
Red lentils – 1/2 cup dry / 100g (Lentil Curry, Red Lentil Porridge)
Green/brown lentils – 1/2 cup / 100g (Lentil Stew)
Chickpeas (cooked or canned) – 1/2 cups / 240g (Spinach Stew, Chickpea Patties, Tapenade Bowl)
White beans – 1/2 cup / 100g (Ratatouille, Stew with Chard)

Dairy & Eggs
Eggs – 10 (Frittata, Poached Egg, Egg Muffins, Scramble)
Greek yogurt – 1 cup / 240ml (Carrot-Oat Pancakes, Orange Yogurt Bowl)
Cottage cheese – 1/2 cup / 120g (Cottage Mousse)
Ricotta cheese – 1/2 cup / 120g (Baked Ricotta, Ricotta Cream)
Feta cheese – 1/2 cup crumbled / 100g (Pancakes, Tomato-Feta Salsa)
Parmesan cheese – 1/4 cup grated / 25g (Zucchini Frittata)

Fish, Poultry & Meat

Chicken thigh – 1 (Braised Chicken with Olives)
Chicken breast – 1 (Grilled Chicken with Bulgur)
Ground turkey – 1/2 lb / 225g (Turkey Meatballs)
Salmon fillet – 1 (Grilled Salmon)
Cod fillet – 1 (Baked Cod, Cod with Garlic Mash)
Shrimp – 6 oz / 170g (Shrimp Skillet, Stir-Fry)

Pantry & Oils

Olive oil – 1/2 cup / 120ml (used throughout)
Almond butter – 1 tbsp (Millet Porridge)
Sunflower seeds – 1 tbsp (Buckwheat Bowl)
Pumpkin seeds – 1 tbsp (Oats with Baked Peach)
Chia seeds – 1 tbsp (Chia Pudding)
Flaxseed – 1 tbsp (Oatmeal with Pear)
Walnuts – 2 tbsp (Ricotta-Fig Bowl, Labneh Dish)
Almonds (sliced or crushed) – 2 tbsp (Carrot-Oat Pancakes, Honey-Apple Boats)
Hazelnuts – 1 tbsp (Ricotta-Fig Bowl)
Sesame seeds – 1 tbsp (Sesame Yogurt, Pear Crumble)
Spices: cinnamon, smoked paprika, cumin, turmeric, thyme, rosemary, black pepper, salt
Herbs: fresh or dried parsley, dill, basil, mint, oregano

Other

Tomato paste – 1 tbsp (Eggplant Bake)
Yogurt-based dip or plain yogurt for drizzle – 1/2 cup (Pancakes, Patties)
Tapenade (or olives + capers) – small jar or 4 tbsp (Tapenade Bowl, Stir-Fry)
Baking powder – 1 tsp (Carrot-Oat Pancakes)
Vanilla extract – 1 tsp (Chia Pudding, Baked Ricotta)

Grocery Shopping List for 8-14 Day Meal Plan

Vegetables

Zucchini – 3 medium (Breakfast Risotto, Falafel Bowl, Quinoa Bowl)
Carrot – 4 medium (Lentil Stew, Quinoa Bowl, Date-Almond Couscous)
Cauliflower – 1 small head (Cauliflower Mash, Cauliflower Curry)
Sweet potato – 2 medium (Baked Cod, Sweet Potato Stew)
Spinach – 5 cups / 150g (Turkey Pilaf, Cannellini Stew, Chicken-Eggplant Sauté)
Swiss chard – 1 cup chopped / 30g (Bean Sauté)
Eggplant – 2 small (Eggplant Bake, Chicken-Eggplant Dish, Eggplant Ragout)
Tomatoes – 4 medium (Egg Skillet, Ratatouille, Tomato Salsa)
Cherry tomatoes – 1 cup / 150g (Polenta with Roasted Tomatoes)
Bell peppers – 3 (Ragout, Chicken Skillet, Shrimp Skillet)
Leeks – 1 stalk (Lentil Bowl)
Red onion – 2 small (Salmon Couscous, Mackerel Salad)
Yellow onion – 2 medium (Chard Sauté, Lentil Stew)
Green beans – 1 cup / 120g (Cod with Garlic Mash)
Cucumber – 1 (Cucumber Boats)
Garlic – 1 bulb (Ratatouille, Falafel, Shrimp Skillet)
Celery – 1 stalk (Lentil Stew)
Pumpkin (or squash) – 1 cup cubed / 150g (Roasted Pumpkin Bowl)
Broccoli – 1 small head (Salmon Couscous)

Fruits

Apples – 2 (Apple-Millet Cream, Apple Boats)
Peach – 1 (Caramelized Peach Halves)
Pear – 2 (Pear Crumble, Warm Pear Delight)
Orange – 1 (Pumpkin Yogurt Bowl)
Lemon – 4 (Salmon, Chicken, Quinoa Bowl, Couscous)
Dates (pitted) – 6 (Mousse, Couscous Cups, Lentil Purée)
Figs (fresh or dried) – 2 (Ricotta Bowl, Fig Cream)
Banana – 2 (Banana Custard, Banana Cake)
Plum – 1 (Roasted Plum Parcel)
Grapes – 1 cup / 150g (Roasted Grapes, Grape Compote)
Pomegranate seeds – 2 tbsp (Pumpkin Yogurt Bowl)

Grains & Legumes

Bulgur – 1/2 cup dry / 90g (Turkey Pilaf, Grilled Chicken Salad)
Farro – 1/2 cup dry / 90g (Lentil-Farro Bowl)
Barley – 1/4 cup dry / 50g (Breakfast Risotto)
Quinoa – 3/4 cup dry / 135g (Quinoa Bowl, Falafel Bowl)
Whole grain couscous – 1/2 cup dry / 90g (Salmon Couscous, Chicken Skillet, Trout Dish)
Wild rice – 1/3 cup dry / 60g (Wild Rice Eggplant Bowl)
Brown rice – 1/3 cup dry / 60g (Stuffed Peppers, Curry)
Millet – 1/4 cup dry / 50g (Millet Cream)
Lentils (green or brown) – 1 cup / 200g (Stew, Lentil Salad)
Red lentils – 1/2 cup / 100g (Red Lentil Porridge)
Chickpeas (cooked or canned) – 1 1/2 cups / 240g (Tagine, Chickpea Patties, Cucumber Boats)
White beans – 1/2 cup / 100g (Ratatouille, Bean Sauté)
Cannellini beans – 1/2 cup / 100g (Stew with Spinach)

Grocery Shopping List for 15-21 Day Meal Plan

Dairy & Eggs
Eggs – 9 (Breakfast Risotto, Egg Skillet, Poached Eggs, Bakes)
Greek yogurt – 1 cup / 240ml (Pumpkin Bowl, Yogurt Drizzle)
Ricotta cheese – 1/2 cup / 120g (Ricotta Cream, Plum Parcel)
Cottage cheese – 1/2 cup / 120g (Vanilla Cottage Cream, Mousse)
Feta cheese – 1/2 cup / 100g (Pumpkin Bowl, Cauliflower Bake, Salsa)
Parmesan cheese – 1/4 cup grated / 25g (Zucchini Frittata)
Goat cheese – 2 tbsp (Roasted Grapes with Goat Cheese)
Labneh or thick yogurt – 1/2 cup (Grilled Veggies)

Fish, Poultry & Meat
Chicken breast – 1 (Chicken Skillet, Couscous Bowl)
Chicken thigh – 1 (Lemon Chicken, Chickpea Bowl)
Ground turkey – 1/2 lb / 225g (Stuffed Peppers)
Cod fillet – 1 (Cod with Garlic Mash)
Mackerel fillet – 1 (Mackerel Salad)
Shrimp – 6 oz / 170g (Shrimp Skillet)
Trout fillet – 1 (Trout with Couscous)

Pantry & Oils
Olive oil – 1/2 cup / 120ml (used throughout)
Almonds – 2 tbsp (Baked Apples, Apple Boats)
Pumpkin seeds – 1 tbsp (Oats or Yogurt)
Sunflower seeds – 1 tbsp (Pumpkin Bowl)
Chia seeds – 1 tbsp (Chia Pudding)
Flaxseed – 1 tbsp (Oatmeal)
Walnuts – 2 tbsp (Roasted Grapes, Ricotta Bowl)
Hazelnuts – 1 tbsp (Ricotta Bowl)
Tahini – 2 tbsp (Lentil Bowl, Veggie Bowl)
Sesame seeds – 1 tbsp (Peach Halves, Sesame Crumble)
Herbs: parsley, thyme, mint, dill, oregano, basil, rosemary
Spices: paprika, cinnamon, cumin, turmeric, black pepper, salt
Rose water – 1 tsp (Lentil-Date Purée)
Vanilla extract – 1 tsp (Baked Ricotta, Banana Cake)
Baking powder – 1 tsp (Banana Cake, Pancakes)
Balsamic vinegar – 1 tbsp (Balsamic Figs)
Tomato paste – 2 tbsp (Eggplant Bake, Shrimp Skillet)
Tapenade or chopped olives – 4 tbsp (Cucumber Boats, Chicken Salad)

Vegetables
Zucchini – 3 medium (Zucchini-Farro Boats, Quinoa Bowl, Lemon Chicken Skillet)
Carrot – 4 medium (Lentil-Carrot Stew, Chickpea Tagine, Apple Bites)
Cauliflower – 1 small head (Cauliflower Mash, Curry with Peas, Quinoa Bowl)
Sweet potato – 2 medium (Sweet Potato Stew, Baked Cod)
Spinach – 5 cups / 150g (Cannellini Stew, Turkey Pilaf, Swiss Chard Sauté)
Swiss chard – 1 cup chopped / 30g (Bean Sauté)
Eggplant – 2 small (Braised Eggplant, Chicken-Eggplant Dish)
Tomatoes – 4 medium (Egg Skillet, Ratatouille, Salsa)
Cherry tomatoes – 1 cup / 150g (Polenta with Tomatoes)
Bell peppers – 3 (Skillet, Trout Dish, Turkey Couscous)
Red onion – 2 small (Farro Salad, Mackerel Salad)
Yellow onion – 2 medium (Lentil Stew, Eggplant Dish, Chard Sauté)
Leeks – 1 stalk (Lentil-Carrot Bowl)
Green beans – 1 cup / 120g (Cod Fillet with Garlic Mash)
Garlic – 1 bulb (Eggplant Bake, Lentils, Skillet, Baked Cod)
Pumpkin or squash – 1 cup / 150g (Pumpkin with Lentils, Couscous Bowl)
Broccoli – 1 small head (Salmon Couscous, Chicken Bowl)
Cucumber – 1 (Chicken-Arugula Salad)
Arugula – 1 cup / 30g (Salad with Chicken, Couscous)
Peas – 1/2 cup / 80g (Cauliflower-Pea Curry)
Fresh herbs – parsley, mint, dill, thyme, oregano, basil

Fruits
Apples – 2 (Apple Bites, Millet Cream)
Pear – 1 (Pear Crumble)
Peach – 1 (Caramelized Peach Halves)
Banana – 1 (Banana Cake)
Orange – 1 (Pumpkin Yogurt Bowl)
Lemon – 4 (Mackerel, Chicken, Couscous Bowl, Salad)
Dates – 6 (Lentil-Date Purée, Date-Almond Couscous)
Figs (fresh or dried) – 2 (Ricotta Bowl, Fig Cream)
Plum – 1 (Roasted Plum Parcel)
Grapes – 1 cup / 150g (Roasted Grapes, Grape Compote)
Pomegranate seeds – 2 tbsp (Pumpkin Yogurt Bowl)

Grains & Legumes
Farro – 1/2 cup dry / 90g (Farro Salad, Turkey Pilaf, Lentil Bowl)
Quinoa – 3/4 cup dry / 135g (Quinoa Bowl, Falafel Bowl)
Whole grain couscous – 1/2 cup dry / 90g (Trout, Chicken Skillet, Couscous Bowl)
Brown rice – 1/2 cup dry / 90g (Peppers, Curry)

illet – 1/4 cup dry / 50g (Millet
ream)
ulgur – 1/2 cup dry / 90g (Turkey
laf, Bulgur Salad)
arley – 1/4 cup dry / 50g (Barley
laf)
ild rice – 1/3 cup dry / 60g (Wild
ce Eggplant Bowl)
entils (green or brown) – 1 cup /
00g (Stew, Warm Bowl, Chickpea
sh)
ed lentils – 1/2 cup / 100g (Lentil
orridge)
hickpeas (cooked or canned) – 2
ps / 320g (Tagine, Falafel, Bowl,
ouscous Dish)
hite beans – 1/2 cup / 100g
Ratatouille, Swiss Chard Sauté)
annellini beans – 1/2 cup / 100g
tew with Spinach)

airy & Eggs
ggs – 9 (Poached Eggs, Egg
killet, Ricotta Bowl, Fig Cream)
reek yogurt – 1 cup / 240ml
umpkin Bowl, Yogurt Drizzle,
ogurt Dip)
cotta cheese – 1/2 cup / 120g
Ricotta Cream, Plum Parcel)
ottage cheese – 1/2 cup / 120g
anilla Cottage Cream)
eta cheese – 1/2 cup / 100g
umpkin Bowl, Cauliflower Bake)
oat cheese – 2 tbsp (Roasted
rapes)
armesan cheese – 1/4 cup grated
25g (Zucchini Frittata)
abneh or thick yogurt – 1/2 cup
Grilled Veggies)

sh, Poultry & Meat
hicken breast – 1 (Grilled
hicken Salad, Couscous Bowl)
hicken thigh – 1 (Braised
hicken)
round turkey – 1/2 lb / 225g
tuffed Peppers, Turkey Pilaf)
od fillet – 1 (Garlic Chickpeas &
pinach, Cod with Mash)
hrimp – 6 oz / 170g (Shrimp
killet)

Mackerel fillet – 1 (Mackerel with Warm Lentil Salad)
Sardines – 1 small tin or 1 fillet (Grilled Sardines)
Trout fillet – 1 (Trout with Couscous)

Pantry & Oils
Olive oil – 1/2 cup / 120ml (used in most dishes)
Almonds – 2 tbsp (Apple Bites, Apple Boats)
Pumpkin seeds – 1 tbsp (Yogurt topping)
Sunflower seeds – 1 tbsp (Pumpkin Bowl)
Chia seeds – 1 tbsp (Chia Pudding)
Flaxseed – 1 tbsp (Oatmeal)
Walnuts – 2 tbsp (Grilled Veggies, Ricotta Bowl)
Hazelnuts – 1 tbsp (Ricotta-Fig Bowl)
Sesame seeds – 1 tbsp (Peach Halves, Pear Crumble)
Tahini – 2 tbsp (Lentil Bowl, Tahini Drizzle)
Spices: paprika, cinnamon, cumin, turmeric, black pepper, salt
Rose water – 1 tsp (Lentil-Date Purée)
Baking powder – 1 tsp (Banana Cake, Pancakes)
Vanilla extract – 1 tsp (Ricotta, Banana Cake)
Tomato paste – 1–2 tbsp (Eggplant Dish, Shrimp Skillet)

Grocery Shopping List for 22-30 Day Meal Plan

Vegetables
Zucchini – 3 medium (Zucchini-Farro Boats, Quinoa Bowl, Lemon Chicken Skillet)
Carrot – 4 medium (Sweet Potato Stew, Lentil-Carrot Bowl, Apple Bites)
Cauliflower – 1 small head (Cauliflower Mash, Cauliflower-Pea Curry)

Sweet potato – 2 medium (Stew, Baked Cod)
Spinach – 5 cups / 150g (Cannellini Stew, Swiss Chard Sauté, Chicken-Eggplant Sauté)
Swiss chard – 1 cup chopped / 30g (White Bean Sauté)
Eggplant – 2 small (Braised Eggplant, Chicken-Eggplant Dish, Eggplant Bake)
Tomatoes – 4 medium (Egg Skillet, Ratatouille, Tomato Salsa, Couscous Bowl)
Cherry tomatoes – 1 cup / 150g (Polenta with Tomatoes)
Bell peppers – 3 (Stuffed Peppers, Shrimp Skillet, Chicken Skillet)
Red onion – 2 small (Farro Salad, Mackerel Lentil Salad)
Yellow onion – 2 medium (Swiss Chard Sauté, Ratatouille, Cod Mash)
Green beans – 1 cup / 120g (Cod Fillet with Mash)
Leeks – 1 stalk (Lentil-Carrot Bowl)
Garlic – 1 bulb (used throughout: Eggplant Bake, Shrimp Skillet, Tagine, White Beans)
Cucumber – 1 (Tuna Boats)
Pumpkin or squash – 1 cup / 150g (Roasted Pumpkin Bowl, Couscous Dish)
Broccoli – 1 small head (Salmon Couscous)
Peas – 1/2 cup / 80g (Curry with Cauliflower)
Fresh herbs – parsley, mint, thyme, dill, basil, oregano

Fruits
Apples – 2 (Apple Bites, Apple Boats)
Pear – 2 (Pear Crumble, Warm Pear Delight)
Peach – 2 (Caramelized Peach, Baked Peach Halves)
Banana – 2 (Banana Custard, Banana Cake)
Orange – 1 (Pumpkin Yogurt Bowl)
Lemon – 4 (Mackerel, Chicken, Couscous Bowl, Yogurt Sauce)

Dates – 6 (Lentil-Date Purée, Quinoa Dessert, Couscous Cups)
Figs (fresh or dried) – 2 (Ricotta Bowl, Fig Cream)
Plum – 1 (Roasted Plum Parcel)
Grapes – 1 cup / 150g (Roasted Grapes, Grape Compote)
Pomegranate seeds – 2 tbsp (Pumpkin Yogurt Bowl)

Grains & Legumes
Quinoa – 3/4 cup dry / 135g (Quinoa Bowl, Falafel Bowl, Quinoa Dessert)
Farro – 1/2 cup dry / 90g (Farro Salad, Turkey Pilaf, Lentil Bowl)
Bulgur – 1/2 cup dry / 90g (Bulgur Salad, Turkey Pilaf, Zucchini Stuffing)
Barley – 1/4 cup dry / 50g (Barley Pilaf, Shrimp Stir-Fry)
Whole grain couscous – 1/2 cup dry / 90g (Trout, Chicken Skillet, Couscous Bowl)
Brown rice – 1/2 cup dry / 90g (Stuffed Peppers, Curry)
Wild rice – 1/3 cup dry / 60g (Wild Rice Eggplant Bowl)
Millet – 1/4 cup dry / 50g (Millet Cream)
Lentils (green or brown) – 1 cup / 200g (Lentil Stew, Carrot Bowl, Chicken Bowl)
Red lentils – 1/2 cup / 100g (Red Lentil Porridge)
Chickpeas (cooked or canned) – 2 cups / 320g (Tagine, Couscous Dish, Chickpea Patties)
White beans – 1/2 cup / 100g (Ratatouille, White Bean Sauté)
Cannellini beans – 1/2 cup / 100g (Spinach Stew)
Dairy & Eggs
Eggs – 9 (Egg Skillet, Poached Eggs, Ricotta Bowl, Eggplant Bakes)
Greek yogurt – 1 cup / 240ml (Yogurt Drizzle, Yogurt Dip, Pumpkin Bowl)
Ricotta cheese – 1/2 cup / 120g (Ricotta Cream, Plum Parcel)

Cottage cheese – 1/2 cup / 120g (Vanilla Cottage Cream, Apple Boats)
Feta cheese – 1/2 cup / 100g (Pumpkin Bowl, Cauliflower Bake, Salsa)
Goat cheese – 2 tbsp (Roasted Grapes with Goat Cheese)
Parmesan cheese – 1/4 cup grated / 25g (Zucchini Frittata)
Labneh or thick yogurt – 1/2 cup (Grilled Veggies)

Fish, Poultry & Meat
Chicken breast – 1 (Grilled Chicken Salad, Couscous Bowl)
Chicken thigh – 1 (Braised Chicken with Olives)
Ground turkey – 1/2 lb / 225g (Stuffed Peppers, Turkey Pilaf)
Cod fillet – 1 (Baked Cod, Cod with Garlic Mash)
Shrimp – 6 oz / 170g (Shrimp Skillet)
Mackerel fillet – 1 (Mackerel with Lentil Salad)
Sardines – 1 tin or fillet (Grilled Sardines)
Trout fillet – 1 (Trout with Couscous)
Pantry & Oils
Olive oil – 1/2 cup / 120ml (used throughout)
Almonds – 2 tbsp (Apple Boats, Caramelized Peach)
Pumpkin seeds – 1 tbsp (Yogurt topping)
Sunflower seeds – 1 tbsp (Pumpkin Bowl)
Chia seeds – 1 tbsp (Chia Pudding)
Flaxseed – 1 tbsp (Oatmeal or Yogurt)
Walnuts – 2 tbsp (Labneh Dish, Ricotta Bowl)
Hazelnuts – 1 tbsp (Ricotta-Fig Bowl)
Sesame seeds – 1 tbsp (Peach Halves, Pear Crumble)
Tahini – 2 tbsp (Lentil Bowl, Vegetable Bowl)

Spices: paprika, cinnamon, cumin, turmeric, black pepper, salt
Rose water – 1 tsp (Lentil-Date Purée)
Baking powder – 1 tsp (Banana Cake, Pancakes)
Vanilla extract – 1 tsp (Chia Pudding, Ricotta)
Balsamic vinegar – 1 tbsp (Balsamic Figs)
Tomato paste – 1–2 tbsp (Eggplant, Salsa, Skillet)

CHAPTER 3: BREAKFAST: Warm & Wholesome Mornings

QUINOA BREAKFAST BOWL WITH BERRIES AND ALMONDS

DIFFICULTY LEVEL: ★☆☆ (EASY) | PREP: 5 MIN | COOK: 15 MIN | SERVES: 1

Ingredients

- 50g (1.8 oz) cooked quinoa
- 80g (2.8 oz) mixed berries (blueberries, raspberries, strawberries)
- 15g (0.5 oz) sliced almonds
- 100g (3.5 oz) plain Greek yogurt (2% fat)
- 1 tsp honey (7g)
- 1/4 tsp cinnamon (0.5g)

Instructions:

1. Cook quinoa according to package instructions and let it cool slightly.
2. In a serving bowl, layer quinoa and yogurt.
3. Top with mixed berries and sliced almonds.
4. Drizzle with honey and sprinkle with cinnamon.
5. Serve immediately or chilled.

Nutritional Facts (Per Serving): Calories: 342 | Carbs: 32g | Protein: 9g | Fat: 19g | Fiber: 5g | Sodium: 30mg | Sugars: 9g

CAULIFLOWER SCRAMBLE WITH FETA AND OREGANO

DIFFICULTY LEVEL: ★☆☆ (EASY) | PREP: 5 MIN | COOK: 10 MIN | SERVES: 1

Ingredients

- 150g (5.3 oz) cauliflower florets, finely chopped
- 2 large eggs (100g)
- 20g (0.7 oz) feta cheese, crumbled
- 1 tbsp olive oil (15ml)
- 1/4 tsp dried oregano (0.5g)
- 1/8 tsp salt (0.5g)
- Pinch of black pepper (0.25g)

Instructions:

1. Heat olive oil in a skillet over medium heat.
2. Add cauliflower and sauté for 5 minutes until softened.
3. Whisk eggs and pour into the skillet, stirring gently.
4. Cook until eggs are set, then add feta, oregano, salt, and pepper.
5. Stir to combine and serve hot.

Nutritional Facts (Per Serving): Calories: 330 | Carbs: 8g | Protein: 16g | Fat: 26g | Fiber: 3g | Sodium: 390mg | Sugars: 3g

WARM APPLE-CINNAMON MILLET WITH WALNUTS

Nutritional Facts (Per Serving): Calories: 348 | Carbs: 39g | Protein: 7g | Fat: 17g | Fiber: 5g | Sodium: 20mg | Sugars: 10g

DIFFICULTY LEVEL: ★☆☆ (EASY) | PREP: 5 MIN | COOK: 15 MIN | SERVES: 1

Ingredients

- 50g (1.8 oz) cooked millet
- 80g (2.8 oz) apple, diced
- 10g (0.35 oz) chopped walnuts
- 100ml (3.4 fl oz) unsweetened almond milk
- 1 tsp maple syrup (7g)
- 1/4 tsp cinnamon (0.5g)

Instructions:

1. In a small saucepan, heat almond milk and add cooked millet.
2. Add diced apple and cinnamon; cook on low heat for 5–7 minutes.
3. Stir in maple syrup and simmer for 1 more minute.
4. Transfer to a bowl and top with chopped walnuts.
5. Serve warm.

MEDITERRANEAN EGG SKILLET WITH TOMATO & GREENS

Nutritional Facts (Per Serving): Calories: 335 | Carbs: 10g | Protein: 17g | Fat: 25g | Fiber: 4g | Sodium: 360mg | Sugars: 5g

DIFFICULTY LEVEL: ★☆☆ (EASY) | PREP: 10 MIN | COOK: 10 MIN | SERVES: 1

Ingredients

- 2 large eggs (100g)
- 1 small tomato, diced (80g)
- 50g (1.75 oz) spinach or Swiss chard, chopped
- 15g (0.5 oz) crumbled feta
- 1 tbsp olive oil (15ml)
- 1/8 tsp salt (0.5g)
- Pinch of black pepper (0.25g)
- Pinch of dried oregano (0.25g)

Instructions:

1. Heat olive oil in a skillet over medium heat.
2. Add tomato and cook for 2–3 minutes until soft.
3. Add greens and sauté until wilted.
4. Make small wells in the vegetables and crack in the eggs.
5. Cover and cook for 4–5 minutes until eggs are set.
6. Top with feta, oregano, salt, and pepper. Serve hot.

CARROT-OAT PANCAKES WITH YOGURT DRIZZLE

Nutritional Facts (Per Serving): Calories: 348 | Carbs: 35g | Protein: 11g | Fat: 18g | Fiber: 5g | Sodium: 240mg | Sugars: 7g

DIFFICULTY LEVEL: ★☆☆ (EASY) | PREP: 10 MIN | COOK: 15 MIN | SERVES: 1

Ingredients

- 40g (1.4 oz) rolled oats
- 50g (1.75 oz) carrot, finely grated
- 1 large egg (50g)
- 30g (1 oz) plain Greek yogurt (for batter)
- 1 tbsp olive oil (10ml), divided
- 1/4 tsp baking powder (1g)
- 1/4 tsp cinnamon (0.5g)
- 1 tsp honey (7g)
- 1/8 tsp salt (0.5g)
- 30g (1 oz) plain Greek yogurt (for drizzle)
- 1 tsp lemon juice (5ml)

Instructions:

1. In a bowl, mix oats, grated carrot, egg, 30g yogurt, baking powder, cinnamon, honey, and salt.
2. Heat half of the olive oil in a non-stick skillet over medium heat.
3. Spoon batter into small pancakes and cook 2–3 minutes per side until golden.
4. Repeat with remaining oil and batter.
5. Mix remaining yogurt with lemon juice for drizzle.
6. Serve pancakes warm with yogurt drizzle on top.

RED LENTIL PORRIDGE WITH OLIVE OIL AND HERBS

Nutritional Facts (Per Serving): Calories: 338 | Carbs: 29g | Protein: 15g | Fat: 17g | Fiber: 7g | Sodium: 250mg | Sugars: 2g

DIFFICULTY LEVEL: ★☆☆ (EASY) | PREP: 5 MIN | COOK: 15 MIN | SERVES: 1

Ingredients

- 60g (2.1 oz) red lentils, rinsed
- 250ml (8.5 fl oz) water
- 1 tbsp olive oil (15ml)
- 1/4 tsp ground cumin (0.5g)
- 1/4 tsp dried thyme (0.5g)
- 1/8 tsp salt (0.5g)
- Pinch of black pepper (0.25g)
- 1 tsp lemon juice (5ml)
- Fresh parsley, chopped (optional)

Instructions:

1. In a small pot, combine red lentils and water. Bring to a boil.
2. Reduce heat and simmer for 12–15 minutes until soft and porridge-like.
3. Stir in olive oil, cumin, thyme, salt, and pepper.
4. Add lemon juice and adjust seasoning to taste.
5. Serve warm, topped with chopped parsley if desired.

CHAPTER 4: BREAKFAST: Light Yet Satisfying

GREEK YOGURT BOWL WITH ORANGE SEGMENTS AND PISTACHIOS

DIFFICULTY LEVEL: ★☆☆ (EASY) | **PREP:** 5 MIN | **COOK:** 0 MIN | **SERVES:** 1

Ingredients

- 150g (5.3 oz) plain Greek yogurt (2% fat)
- 1 medium orange, peeled and segmented (130g)
- 10g (0.35 oz) unsalted pistachios, chopped
- 1 tsp honey (7g)
- 1/4 tsp ground cinnamon (0.5g)

Instructions:

1. Place Greek yogurt into a bowl.
2. Top with orange segments and chopped pistachios.
3. Drizzle with honey and sprinkle with cinnamon.
4. Serve immediately.

Nutritional Facts (Per Serving): Calories: 337 | Carbs: 27g | Protein: 18g | Fat: 17g | Fiber: 3g | Sodium: 70mg | Sugars: 21g

BUCKWHEAT WITH STEWED PLUMS AND SUNFLOWER SEEDS

DIFFICULTY LEVEL: ★☆☆ (EASY) | **PREP:** 5 MIN | **COOK:** 15 MIN | **SERVES:** 1

Ingredients

- 50g (1.75 oz) cooked buckwheat
- 100g (3.5 oz) ripe plums, sliced
- 1 tsp maple syrup (7g)
- 10g (0.35 oz) sunflower seeds
- 1 tsp olive oil (5ml)
- 1/4 tsp cinnamon (0.5g)

Instructions:

1. Simmer sliced plums with maple syrup and cinnamon for 5–7 minutes until soft and syrupy.
2. Warm the cooked buckwheat in a pan with olive oil.
3. Transfer buckwheat to a bowl and top with stewed plums.
4. Sprinkle with sunflower seeds and serve warm.

Nutritional Facts (Per Serving): Calories: 345 | Carbs: 38g | Protein: 8g | Fat: 17g | Fiber: 5g | Sodium: 15mg | Sugars: 14g

BAKED RICOTTA WITH ROASTED STRAWBERRIES

DIFFICULTY LEVEL: ★☆☆ (EASY) | PREP: 5 MIN | COOK: 20 MIN | SERVES: 1

Ingredients

- 100g (3.5 oz) ricotta cheese
- 80g (2.8 oz) fresh strawberries, halved
- 1 tsp olive oil (5ml)
- 1 tsp honey (7g)
- 1/4 tsp vanilla extract (1ml)

Instructions:

1. Preheat oven to 180°C (350°F).
2. Place ricotta into a small ramekin and bake for 15 minutes.
3. Toss strawberries with olive oil and vanilla; roast separately for 10–12 minutes.
4. Top the baked ricotta with warm roasted strawberries.
5. Drizzle with honey and serve warm or at room temperature.

Nutritional Facts (Per Serving): Calories: 343 | Carbs: 21g | Protein: 15g | Fat: 22g | Fiber: 3g | Sodium: 180mg | Sugars: 16g

MUSHROOM-EGG STIR WITH THYME AND BABY SPINACH

DIFFICULTY LEVEL: ★☆☆ (EASY) | PREP: 5 MIN | COOK: 10 MIN | SERVES: 1

Ingredients

- 2 large eggs (100g)
- 80g (2.8 oz) mushrooms, sliced
- 40g (1.4 oz) baby spinach
- 1 tbsp olive oil (15ml)
- 1/4 tsp dried thyme (0.5g)
- 1/8 tsp salt (0.5g)
- Pinch of black pepper (0.25g)

Instructions:

1. Heat olive oil in a skillet over medium heat.
2. Sauté mushrooms for 5–6 minutes until golden.
3. Add spinach and thyme; cook until wilted.
4. Whisk eggs, then pour into skillet and stir constantly.
5. Season with salt and pepper. Serve hot.

Nutritional Facts (Per Serving): Calories: 345 | Carbs: 7g | Protein: 18g | Fat: 26g | Fiber: 3g | Sodium: 260mg | Sugars: 3g

PUMPKIN PUREE PORRIDGE WITH CINNAMON AND CHIA

DIFFICULTY LEVEL: ★☆☆ (EASY) | **PREP:** 5 MIN | **COOK:** 10 MIN | **SERVES:** 1

Ingredients

- 40g (1.4 oz) rolled oats
- 100ml (3.4 fl oz) unsweetened almond milk
- 80g (2.8 oz) pumpkin purée
- 1 tsp chia seeds (5g)
- 1 tsp maple syrup (7g)
- 1/2 tsp cinnamon (1g)
- 1 tsp olive oil (5ml)
- Pinch of salt (0.25g)

Instructions:

1. In a small saucepan, combine oats, almond milk, pumpkin purée, cinnamon, and salt.
2. Simmer for 6–8 minutes, stirring occasionally.
3. Stir in chia seeds and olive oil.
4. Cook for another 2 minutes until thickened.
5. Transfer to a bowl and drizzle with maple syrup. Serve warm.

Nutritional Facts (Per Serving): Calories: 344 | Carbs: 32g | Protein: 8g | Fat: 20g | Fiber: 6g | Sodium: 40mg | Sugars: 9g

OATMEAL WITH PEAR, FLAXSEED, AND CRUSHED ALMONDS

DIFFICULTY LEVEL: ★☆☆ (EASY) | **PREP:** 5 MIN | **COOK:** 10 MIN | **SERVES:** 1

Ingredients

- 40g (1.4 oz) rolled oats
- 100ml (3.4 fl oz) unsweetened oat milk
- 80g (2.8 oz) ripe pear, diced
- 1 tsp ground flaxseed (3g)
- 1 tsp crushed almonds (5g)
- 1 tsp honey (7g)
- 1/4 tsp cinnamon (0.5g)

Instructions:

1. Cook oats with oat milk over medium heat for 5–6 minutes.
2. Add diced pear and continue cooking for 2–3 minutes.
3. Stir in flaxseed and cinnamon.
4. Transfer to a bowl and top with honey and crushed almonds.
5. Serve warm.

Nutritional Facts (Per Serving): Calories: 342 | Carbs: 36g | Protein: 7g | Fat: 18g | Fiber: 6g | Sodium: 20mg | Sugars: 10g

COTTAGE CHEESE WITH STEAMED APPLES AND POPPY SEEDS

DIFFICULTY LEVEL: ★☆☆ (EASY) | PREP: 5 MIN | COOK: 5 MIN | SERVES: 1

Ingredients

- 120g (4.2 oz) low-fat cottage cheese
- 80g (2.8 oz) apple, peeled and diced
- 1 tsp olive oil (5ml)
- 1 tsp poppy seeds (3g)
- 1 tsp maple syrup (7g)
- 1/4 tsp cinnamon (0.5g)

Instructions:

1. Steam diced apple for 3–4 minutes until tender.
2. Place cottage cheese in a serving bowl.
3. Top with steamed apples and drizzle with olive oil and maple syrup.
4. Sprinkle with poppy seeds and cinnamon.
5. Serve warm or at room temperature.

Nutritional Facts (Per Serving): Calories: 335 | Carbs: 26g | Protein: 16g | Fat: 18g | Fiber: 4g | Sodium: 280mg | Sugars: 11g

VEGETABLE MEDLEY BAKE WITH EGG AND BASIL

DIFFICULTY LEVEL: ★☆☆ (EASY) | PREP: 10 MIN | COOK: 20 MIN | SERVES: 1

Ingredients

- 1 large egg (50g)
- 60g (2.1 oz) zucchini, chopped
- 50g (1.75 oz) red bell pepper, chopped
- 40g (1.4 oz) cherry tomatoes, halved
- 20g (0.7 oz) onion, chopped
- 1 tbsp grated Parmesan (8g)
- 1 tbsp olive oil (15ml)
- 1 tbsp chopped fresh basil (5g)
- 1/8 tsp salt (0.5g)
- Pinch of black pepper (0.25g)

Instructions:

1. Preheat oven to 180°C (350°F).
2. Toss vegetables with olive oil, salt, and pepper.
3. Transfer to a small baking dish and bake for 10 minutes.
4. Crack egg over the vegetables and sprinkle with Parmesan.
5. Bake for another 10 minutes until the egg is set.
6. Top with fresh basil and serve hot.

Nutritional Facts (Per Serving): Calories: 349 | Carbs: 12g | Protein: 16g | Fat: 26g | Fiber: 4g | Sodium: 300mg | Sugars: 6g

CHAPTER 5: BREAKFAST: Comfort Bowls

MILLET PORRIDGE WITH DRIED APRICOTS AND ALMOND BUTTER

DIFFICULTY LEVEL: ★☆☆ (EASY) | PREP: 5 MIN | COOK: 15 MIN | SERVES: 1

Ingredients

- 50g (1.75 oz) cooked millet
- 3 dried apricots, chopped (20g)
- 1 tbsp almond butter (16g)
- 100ml (3.4 fl oz) unsweetened almond milk
- 1/4 tsp cinnamon (0.5g)
- 1/2 tsp honey (3g)

Instructions:

1. Warm the almond milk in a saucepan over medium heat.
2. Add cooked millet, dried apricots, and cinnamon.
3. Simmer for 5–7 minutes, stirring occasionally.
4. Stir in almond butter and cook 1 more minute.
5. Transfer to a bowl and drizzle with honey before serving.

Nutritional Facts (Per Serving): Calories: 345 | Carbs: 36g | Protein: 7g | Fat: 18g | Fiber: 4g | Sodium: 15mg | Sugars: 10g

SCRAMBLED EGGS WITH SAUTÉED KALE AND RED ONION

DIFFICULTY LEVEL: ★☆☆ (EASY) | PREP: 5 MIN | COOK: 10 MIN | SERVES: 1

Ingredients

- 2 large eggs (100g)
- 60g (2.1 oz) kale, chopped
- 30g (1 oz) red onion, sliced
- 1 tbsp olive oil (15ml)
- 1/4 tsp garlic powder (0.5g)
- 1/8 tsp salt (0.5g)
- Pinch of black pepper (0.25g)

Instructions:

1. Heat half the olive oil in a skillet over medium heat.
2. Sauté red onion for 2–3 minutes until softened.
3. Add kale and garlic powder; cook until wilted.
4. Whisk eggs and pour into the skillet.
5. Scramble gently until just set.
6. Season with salt, pepper, and drizzle remaining oil.

Nutritional Facts (Per Serving): Calories: 343 | Carbs: 8g | Protein: 17g | Fat: 26g | Fiber: 3g | Sodium: 320mg | Sugars: 3g

RICE & CHICKPEA BOWL WITH OLIVE TAPENADE CRUMBLE

DIFFICULTY LEVEL: ★☆☆ (EASY) | **PREP:** 10 MIN | **COOK:** 10 MIN | **SERVES:** 1

Ingredients

- 60g (2.1 oz) cooked brown rice
- 70g (2.5 oz) cooked chickpeas
- 10g (0.35 oz) black olive tapenade
- 1 tbsp lemon juice (15ml)
- 1 tbsp olive oil (15ml)
- 1 tbsp chopped parsley (5g)
- 1/8 tsp salt (0.5g)
- Pinch of cumin (0.25g)

Instructions:

1. In a bowl, mix chickpeas, rice, olive oil, lemon juice, cumin, and salt.
2. Stir gently until well combined.
3. Top with olive tapenade and chopped parsley.
4. Serve warm or room temperature.

Nutritional Facts (Per Serving): Calories: 348 | Carbs: 38g | Protein: 10g | Fat: 17g | Fiber: 6g | Sodium: 360mg | Sugars: 3g

ZUCCHINI-CARROT PANCAKES WITH YOGURT-HERB DIP

DIFFICULTY LEVEL: ★☆☆ (EASY) | **PREP:** 10 MIN | **COOK:** 15 MIN | **SERVES:** 1

Ingredients

- 50g (1.75 oz) zucchini, grated
- 40g (1.4 oz) carrot, grated
- 1 large egg (50g)
- 1 tbsp almond flour (10g)
- 1 tbsp olive oil (15ml)
- Pinch of salt and pepper

For the dip:
- 50g (1.75 oz) plain Greek yogurt
- 1 tsp lemon juice (5ml)
- 1 tsp chopped dill or parsley (2g)

Instructions:

1. Squeeze moisture from grated zucchini and carrot.
2. In a bowl, mix vegetables with egg, almond flour, salt, and pepper.
3. Heat oil in a skillet and fry small pancakes 2–3 minutes per side.
4. In a small bowl, mix yogurt, lemon juice, and herbs.
5. Serve pancakes warm with yogurt-herb dip on the side.

Nutritional Facts (Per Serving): Calories: 346 | Carbs: 20g | Protein: 11g | Fat: 24g | Fiber: 4g | Sodium: 310mg | Sugars: 7g

APPLE-WALNUT FARRO WITH GREEK YOGURT CREAM

DIFFICULTY LEVEL: ★☆☆ (EASY) | **PREP:** 5 MIN | **COOK:** 15 MIN | **SERVES:** 1

Ingredients

- 60g (2.1 oz) cooked farro
- 80g (2.8 oz) apple, diced
- 10g (0.35 oz) walnuts, chopped
- 1/4 tsp cinnamon (0.5g)
- 1 tsp honey (7g)
- 60g (2.1 oz) plain Greek yogurt (for topping)

Instructions:

1. In a small saucepan, warm the cooked farro and apple over low heat for 5 minutes.
2. Stir in cinnamon and honey.
3. Transfer to a bowl and top with chopped walnuts.
4. Spoon yogurt on top and serve warm.

Nutritional Facts (Per Serving): Calories: 345 | Carbs: 36g | Protein: 9g | Fat: 18g | Fiber: 4g | Sodium: 40mg | Sugars: 12g

MASHED SWEET POTATO WITH POACHED EGG AND DILL

DIFFICULTY LEVEL: ★☆☆ (EASY) | **PREP:** 10 MIN | **COOK:** 15 MIN | **SERVES:** 1

Ingredients

- 100g (3.5 oz) sweet potato, peeled and cubed
- 1 large egg (50g)
- 1 tbsp olive oil (15ml)
- 1 tsp lemon juice (5ml)
- 1 tsp chopped fresh dill (2g)
- 1/8 tsp salt (0.5g)
- Pinch of black pepper (0.25g)

Instructions:

1. Boil or steam sweet potato cubes until tender (10–12 minutes), then mash with olive oil, salt, and pepper.
2. Poach egg in simmering water with vinegar for 3–4 minutes.
3. Spoon mashed sweet potato onto a plate and top with poached egg.
4. Drizzle with lemon juice and sprinkle with fresh dill.
5. Serve immediately.

Nutritional Facts (Per Serving): Calories: 334 | Carbs: 25g | Protein: 10g | Fat: 20g | Fiber: 4g | Sodium: 210mg | Sugars: 6g

OATS WITH BAKED PEACH AND PUMPKIN SEEDS

DIFFICULTY LEVEL: ★☆☆ (EASY) | **PREP:** 5 MIN | **COOK:** 20 MIN | **SERVES:** 1

Ingredients

- 40g (1.4 oz) rolled oats
- 100ml (3.4 fl oz) unsweetened almond milk
- 1 medium peach, sliced (100g)
- 1 tsp olive oil (5ml)
- 1 tsp maple syrup (7g)
- 1 tsp pumpkin seeds (5g)
- 1/4 tsp cinnamon (0.5g)

Instructions:

1. Preheat oven to 180°C (350°F).
2. Toss peach slices with olive oil and cinnamon. Bake for 15 minutes.
3. In a saucepan, cook oats with almond milk for 5–7 minutes until creamy.
4. Spoon oatmeal into a bowl, top with baked peach slices.
5. Drizzle with maple syrup and sprinkle with pumpkin seeds.

Nutritional Facts (Per Serving): Calories: 348 | Carbs: 36g | Protein: 9g | Fat: 18g | Fiber: 5g | Sodium: 15mg | Sugars: 11g

SPINACH-TOMATO EGG MUFFINS (BAKED STYLE)

DIFFICULTY LEVEL: ★☆☆ (EASY) | **PREP:** 10 MIN | **COOK:** 20 MIN | **SERVES:** 1

Ingredients

- 2 large eggs (100g)
- 50g (1.75 oz) fresh spinach, chopped
- 40g (1.4 oz) cherry tomatoes, halved
- 15g (0.5 oz) shredded cheese (e.g., mozzarella or cheddar)
- 1 tbsp olive oil (15ml)
- 1/8 tsp salt (0.5g)
- Pinch of black pepper (0.25g)

Instructions:

1. Preheat oven to 180°C (350°F). Lightly grease a muffin tin with oil.
2. Whisk eggs in a bowl with salt and pepper.
3. Stir in spinach, tomatoes, and cheese.
4. Pour mixture into 2 muffin molds.
5. Bake for 18–20 minutes or until set and slightly golden.
6. Let cool slightly before serving.

Nutritional Facts (Per Serving): Calories: 338 | Carbs: 6g | Protein: 20g | Fat: 26g | Fiber: 2g | Sodium: 390mg | Sugars: 3g

CHAPTER 6: BREAKFAST: Savory Balance

LENTIL & TOMATO STEW WITH SOFT-BOILED EGG

DIFFICULTY LEVEL: ★☆☆ (EASY) | **PREP:** 10 MIN | **COOK:** 15 MIN | **SERVES:** 1

Ingredients

- 60g (2.1 oz) cooked brown lentils
- 100g (3.5 oz) canned diced tomatoes
- 1 large egg (50g)
- 1 tbsp olive oil (15ml)
- 1/2 small onion, chopped (30g)
- 1/4 tsp ground cumin (0.5g)
- 1/4 tsp dried thyme (0.5g)
- 1/8 tsp salt (0.5g)
- Pinch of black pepper (0.25g)

Instructions:

1. In a saucepan, sauté onion in olive oil un translucent.
2. Add lentils, tomatoes, cumin, thyme, salt, ar pepper. Simmer 10 minutes.
3. Soft-boil the egg for 6 minutes, then peel.
4. Serve stew in a bowl topped with halved egg.
5. Optional: garnish with fresh parsley.

Nutritional Facts (Per Serving): Calories: 342 | Carbs: 29g | Protein: 17g | Fat: 17g | Fiber: 7g | Sodium: 310mg | Sugars: 7g

EGGPLANT & BELL PEPPER RAGOUT WITH HERBS

DIFFICULTY LEVEL: ★☆☆ (EASY) | **PREP:** 10 MIN | **COOK:** 20 MIN | **SERVES:** 1

Ingredients

- 80g (2.8 oz) eggplant, diced
- 60g (2.1 oz) red bell pepper, diced
- 50g (1.75 oz) canned chopped tomatoes
- 1/2 small onion, chopped (30g)
- 1 tbsp olive oil (15ml)
- 1/2 tsp dried oregano (1g)
- 1/8 tsp salt (0.5g)
- Pinch of chili flakes (optional)
- Fresh parsley or basil for garnish

Instructions:

1. Heat olive oil in a skillet and sauté onion until soft.
2. Add eggplant and bell pepper; cook for 5–6 minutes
3. Add tomatoes, oregano, salt, and chili flakes. Simm for 10 minutes.
4. Cook until vegetables are tender and flavors meld.
5. Top with chopped herbs and serve warm.

Nutritional Facts (Per Serving): Calories: 339 | Carbs: 22g | Protein: 6g | Fat: 25g | Fiber: 6g | Sodium: 300mg | Sugars: 10g

CHICKPEA & LEEK MASH WITH CUMIN AND PARSLEY

Nutritional Facts (Per Serving): Calories: 340 | Carbs: 28g | Protein: 9g | Fat: 21g | Fiber: 6g | Sodium: 250mg | Sugars: 4g

DIFFICULTY LEVEL: ★☆☆ (EASY) | PREP: 10 MIN | COOK: 15 MIN | SERVES: 1

Ingredients

- 100g (3.5 oz) cooked chickpeas
- 50g (1.75 oz) leek, thinly sliced
- 1 tbsp olive oil (15ml)
- 1 tbsp lemon juice (15ml)
- 1/4 tsp ground cumin (0.5g)
- 1 tbsp chopped fresh parsley (5g)
- 1/8 tsp salt (0.5g)
- Pinch of black pepper (0.25g)

Instructions:

1. Sauté leeks in olive oil over medium heat until softened.
2. Add chickpeas and cumin; cook for 3 minutes.
3. Add lemon juice, salt, and pepper.
4. Mash the mixture roughly with a fork or potato masher.
5. Transfer to a plate and sprinkle with parsley. Serve warm.

BARLEY BREAKFAST RISOTTO WITH ZUCCHINI AND EGG

Nutritional Facts (Per Serving): Calories: 347 | Carbs: 30g | Protein: 13g | Fat: 21g | Fiber: 5g | Sodium: 260mg | Sugars: 4g

DIFFICULTY LEVEL: ★☆☆ (EASY) | PREP: 10 MIN | COOK: 20 MIN | SERVES: 1

Ingredients

- 60g (2.1 oz) cooked pearl barley
- 80g (2.8 oz) zucchini, grated
- 1 large egg (50g)
- 1 tbsp olive oil (15ml)
- 1 tbsp grated Parmesan (7g)
- 1/8 tsp salt (0.5g)
- Pinch of black pepper (0.25g)
- 1/2 tsp dried basil or thyme (0.5g)

Instructions:

1. Heat olive oil in a non-stick pan and sauté zucchini for 3–4 minutes.
2. Add cooked barley, salt, herbs, and pepper; stir to warm through.
3. Mix in grated Parmesan and stir gently.
4. In a separate pan, fry egg sunny side up.
5. Serve risotto in a bowl topped with the egg.
6. Carefully fold the lettuce leaves over the filling, securing the ends like a wrap.

WARM RICOTTA & FIG BOWL WITH CRUSHED HAZELNUTS

DIFFICULTY LEVEL: ★☆☆ (EASY) | **PREP:** 5 MIN | **COOK:** 10 MIN | **SERVES:** 1

Ingredients

- 100g (3.5 oz) ricotta cheese
- 2 fresh figs, sliced (80g)
- 1 tsp honey (7g)
- 1 tsp crushed hazelnuts (5g)
- 1/4 tsp cinnamon (0.5g)

Instructions:

1. Warm ricotta in a small pan or microwave-safe bowl (1–2 minutes until soft but not melted).
2. Top with sliced figs and drizzle with honey.
3. Sprinkle with cinnamon and crushed hazelnuts.
4. Serve immediately while warm.

Nutritional Facts (Per Serving): Calories: 343 | Carbs: 24g | Protein: 14g | Fat: 21g | Fiber: 3g | Sodium: 150mg | Sugars: 16g

STEAMED BROCCOLI WITH EGG AND YOGURT DRESSING

DIFFICULTY LEVEL: ★☆☆ (EASY) | **PREP:** 5 MIN | **COOK:** 10 MIN | **SERVES:** 1

Ingredients

- 120g (4.2 oz) broccoli florets
- 1 large egg (50g)
- 50g (1.75 oz) plain Greek yogurt
- 1 tsp olive oil (5ml)
- 1 tsp lemon juice (5ml)
- 1/8 tsp salt (0.5g)
- Pinch of black pepper (0.25g)
- 1/4 tsp garlic powder (0.5g)

Instructions:

1. Steam broccoli for 6–7 minutes until tender.
2. Soft-boil or poach the egg to desired doneness.
3. In a small bowl, mix yogurt, lemon juice, olive oil, garlic powder, salt, and pepper.
4. Serve broccoli in a bowl topped with egg and drizzle with yogurt dressing.

Nutritional Facts (Per Serving): Calories: 335 | Carbs: 10g | Protein: 16g | Fat: 24g | Fiber: 4g | Sodium: 260mg | Sugars: 4g

CAULIFLOWER MASH WITH POACHED EGG AND OLIVE OIL

DIFFICULTY LEVEL: ★☆☆ (EASY) | **PREP:** 5 MIN | **COOK:** 15 MIN | **SERVES:** 1

Ingredients

- 180g (6.3 oz) cauliflower florets
- 1 large egg (50g)
- 1 tbsp olive oil (15ml)
- 1 tbsp plain Greek yogurt (15g)
- 1/4 tsp garlic powder (0.5g)
- 1/8 tsp salt (0.5g)
- Pinch of black pepper (0.25g)

Instructions:

1. Steam cauliflower until tender (about 10–12 minutes).
2. Blend or mash with yogurt, olive oil, garlic powder, salt, and pepper until creamy.
3. Poach the egg in simmering water for 3–4 minutes.
4. Serve mash in a bowl topped with poached egg and drizzle with extra olive oil if desired.

Nutritional Facts (Per Serving): Calories: 337 | Carbs: 12g | Protein: 13g | Fat: 26g | Fiber: 4g | Sodium: 230mg | Sugars: 4g

ROASTED PUMPKIN WITH FETA AND FRESH THYME

DIFFICULTY LEVEL: ★☆☆ (EASY) | **PREP:** 10 MIN | **COOK:** 25 MIN | **SERVES:** 1

Ingredients

- 150g (5.3 oz) pumpkin, cubed
- 25g (0.9 oz) feta cheese, crumbled
- 1 tbsp olive oil (15ml)
- 1 tsp fresh thyme leaves (1g)
- 1/4 tsp paprika (0.5g)
- 1/8 tsp salt (0.5g)
- Pinch of black pepper (0.25g)

Instructions:

1. Preheat oven to 200°C (400°F).
2. Toss pumpkin with olive oil, paprika, salt, and pepper.
3. Spread on a baking sheet and roast for 20–25 minutes until tender and slightly browned.
4. Transfer to a plate and top with crumbled feta and fresh thyme.
5. Serve warm.

Nutritional Facts (Per Serving): Calories: 340 | Carbs: 19g | Protein: 12g | Fat: 24g | Fiber: 4g | Sodium: 360mg | Sugars: 7g

CHAPTER 7: LUNCH: Earthy & Nourishing Bowls

CHICKPEA & SPINACH STEW WITH ROASTED GARLIC

Nutritional Facts (Per Serving): Calories: 521 | Carbs: 42g | Protein: 18g | Fat: 29g | Fiber: 11g | Sodium: 410mg | Sugars: 7g

DIFFICULTY LEVEL: ★☆☆ (EASY) | **PREP:** 10 MIN | **COOK:** 20 MIN | **SERVES:** 1

Ingredients

- 150g (5.3 oz) cooked chickpeas
- 70g (2.5 oz) fresh spinach, chopped
- 1 small onion, diced (60g)
- 1 medium tomato, diced (120g)
- 3 garlic cloves, whole (15g)
- 1.5 tbsp olive oil (22ml)
- 1/2 tsp ground cumin (1g)
- 1/4 tsp paprika (0.5g)
- 1/4 tsp salt (1g)
- Pinch of black pepper (0.25g)

Instructions:

1. Preheat oven to 200°C (400°F). Wrap garlic cloves foil with a drop of olive oil and roast for 15 minutes.
2. In a pot, heat remaining olive oil and sauté onion f 3–4 minutes.
3. Add chickpeas, tomato, spinach, cumin, paprika, sa and pepper.
4. Squeeze in roasted garlic and simmer for 10–1 minutes.
5. Serve warm, garnished with extra herbs if desired

GRILLED CHICKEN WITH BULGUR AND LEMON-ZUCCHINI

Nutritional Facts (Per Serving): Calories: 498 | Carbs: 37g | Protein: 35g | Fat: 24g | Fiber: 6g | Sodium: 310mg | Sugars: 4g

DIFFICULTY LEVEL: ★☆☆ (EASY) | **PREP:** 10 MIN | **COOK:** 15 MIN | **SERVES:** 1

Ingredients

- 130g (4.6 oz) skinless chicken breast
- 60g (2.1 oz) dry bulgur
- 100g (3.5 oz) zucchini, diced
- 1 tbsp olive oil (15ml)
- 1 tbsp lemon juice (15ml)
- 1/2 garlic clove, minced (2g
- 1/4 tsp dried oregano (0.5g
- 1/4 tsp salt (1g)
- Pinch of black pepper (0.25g)

Instructions:

1. Season chicken breast with garlic powder, salt, ar pepper. Grill for 5–6 minutes per side until cooke through.
2. Sauté zucchini in olive oil for 5–6 minutes un golden and soft.
3. In a bowl, combine bulgur, sautéed zucchini, lemo juice, and parsley.
4. Slice grilled chicken and serve over the bulg mixture.

RED LENTIL CURRY WITH CARROT AND BROWN RICE

DIFFICULTY LEVEL: ★☆☆ (EASY) | **PREP:** 10 MIN | **COOK:** 20 MIN | **SERVES:** 1

Ingredients

- 70g (2.5 oz) dry red lentils
- 50g (1.8 oz) brown rice
- 80g (2.8 oz) carrot, grated
- 1/2 small onion, diced (40g)
- 1 garlic clove, minced (5g)
- 1/2 tsp curry powder (1g)
- 1/4 tsp turmeric (0.5g)
- 1 tbsp olive oil (15ml)
- 1 cup water (240ml)
- 1/4 tsp salt (1g)
- Pinch of chili flakes (optional)

Instructions:

1. In a saucepan, heat olive oil and add turmeric, curry powder, and carrots.
2. Stir for 2 minutes, then add lentils and water.
3. Simmer for 15–18 minutes until lentils are tender and mixture thickens.
4. Season with salt and pepper.
5. Serve curry over warm brown rice.

Nutritional Facts (Per Serving): Calories: 489 | Carbs: 44g | Protein: 19g | Fat: 24g | Fiber: 9g | Sodium: 360mg | Sugars: 6g

BAKED COD WITH SWEET POTATO AND OLIVE RELISH

DIFFICULTY LEVEL: ★☆☆ (EASY) | **PREP:** 10 MIN | **COOK:** 20 MIN | **SERVES:** 1

Ingredients

- 140g (5 oz) cod fillet
- 100g (3.5 oz) sweet potato, cubed
- 20g (0.7 oz) pitted green olives, chopped
- 1 tbsp olive oil (15ml)
- 1 tsp lemon juice (5ml)
- 1/4 tsp dried oregano (0.5g)
- 1/8 tsp salt (0.5g)
- Pinch of black pepper (0.25g)

Instructions:

1. Preheat oven to 190°C (375°F). Place sweet potatoes on a baking tray, drizzle with half the oil, and roast for 20 minutes.
2. Season cod with salt, pepper, oregano, and remaining oil.
3. Add cod to the tray and bake for 12–15 minutes or until flaky.
4. In a small bowl, mix chopped olives with lemon juice to make a relish.
5. Serve cod over roasted sweet potato and top with olive relish.

Nutritional Facts (Per Serving): Calories: 478 | Carbs: 35g | Protein: 32g | Fat: 24g | Fiber: 5g | Sodium: 410mg | Sugars: 6g

QUINOA BOWL WITH ROASTED VEGETABLES AND FETA

Nutritional Facts (Per Serving): Calories: 528 | Carbs: 42g | Protein: 18g | Fat: 30g | Fiber: 7g | Sodium: 440mg | Sugars: 7g

DIFFICULTY LEVEL: ★☆☆ (EASY) | PREP: 10 MIN | COOK: 25 MIN | SERVES: 1

Ingredients

- 60g (2.1 oz) dry quinoa
- 80g (2.8 oz) zucchini, chopped
- 70g (2.5 oz) red bell pepper, chopped
- 60g (2.1 oz) eggplant, cubed
- 40g (1.4 oz) red onion, sliced
- 40g (1.4 oz) feta cheese, crumbled
- 1.5 tbsp olive oil (22ml)
- 1/2 tsp dried oregano (1g)
- 1/2 tsp lemon zest (1g)
- 1/2 tbsp lemon juice (7ml)
- 1/4 tsp salt (1g)
- Pinch black pepper (0.25g)

Instructions:

1. Preheat oven to 200°C (400°F).
2. Toss zucchini, bell pepper, and eggplant with olive oil, salt, pepper, and oregano.
3. Roast vegetables for 20–25 minutes until tender and golden.
4. Combine roasted vegetables with cooked quinoa.
5. Top with crumbled feta and serve warm or at room temperature.

TURKEY MEATBALLS WITH TOMATO-BARLEY RAGU

Nutritional Facts (Per Serving): Calories: 512 | Carbs: 35g | Protein: 34g | Fat: 26g | Fiber: 6g | Sodium: 460mg | Sugars: 7g

DIFFICULTY LEVEL: ★★☆ (MODERATE) | PREP: 15 MIN | COOK: 20 MIN | SERVES: 1

Ingredients

- 120g (4.2 oz) ground turkey (93% lean)
- 1 tbsp chopped parsley (3g)
- 1/2 garlic clove, minced (2g)
- 1 tbsp grated onion (10g)
- 1/2 tbsp olive oil (7ml)
- Salt & pepper to taste
- **For the ragu:**
- 60g (2.1 oz) pearl barley, dry
- 100g (3.5 oz) canned chopped tomatoes
- 40g (1.4 oz) carrot, grated
- 30g (1 oz) celery, diced
- 1/2 tbsp olive oil (7ml)
- 1/2 garlic clove (2g)
- 1/4 tsp dried thyme (0.5g)
- 1/4 tsp salt (1g)
- Pinch of chili flakes (optional)

Instructions:

1. Cook barley in water (2:1 ratio) for 25–30 minutes until tender.
2. Meanwhile, mix turkey with parsley, grated onion, garlic, salt, and pepper. Form 3–4 meatballs.
3. Heat olive oil in a skillet and brown meatballs on all sides for 6–8 minutes.
4. In another pan, heat olive oil and sauté garlic, carrot, and celery for 5 minutes.
5. Add tomatoes, thyme, salt, chili flakes, and simmer for 10 minutes. Stir in cooked barley.
6. Serve meatballs over tomato-barley ragu.

BROCCOLI & CAULIFLOWER STIR WITH TAHINI-LIME SAUCE

DIFFICULTY LEVEL: ★☆☆ (EASY) | PREP: 10 MIN | COOK: 10 MIN | SERVES: 1

Ingredients

- 100g (3.5 oz) broccoli florets
- 100g (3.5 oz) cauliflower florets
- 1/2 small red onion, sliced (30g)
- 1 tbsp olive oil (15ml)
- 1/4 tsp salt (1g)
- Pinch black pepper (0.25g)
- For sauce:
- 1.5 tbsp tahini (22g)
- 1 tbsp lime juice (15ml)
- 1 tsp soy sauce (5ml)
- 1 tbsp water (15ml)
- 1/2 garlic clove, grated (2g)

Instructions:

1. Steam or lightly boil broccoli and cauliflower for 4–5 minutes until just tender.
2. In a skillet, heat olive oil and sauté onion for 3–4 minutes until soft.
3. Add broccoli and cauliflower, season with salt and pepper, stir-fry 2 minutes.
4. Mix tahini, lime juice, soy sauce, garlic, and water until creamy.
5. Drizzle tahini-lime sauce over the stir-fry and serve immediately.

Nutritional Facts (Per Serving): Calories: 455 | Carbs: 24g | Protein: 14g | Fat: 32g | Fiber: 9g | Sodium: 330mg | Sugars: 6g

WILD RICE WITH MUSHROOMS AND POACHED EGG

DIFFICULTY LEVEL: ★☆☆ (EASY) | PREP: 10 MIN | COOK: 20 MIN | SERVES: 1

Ingredients

- 60g (2.1 oz) dry wild rice
- 100g (3.5 oz) mushrooms, sliced
- 1 large egg (50g)
- 1 tbsp olive oil (15ml)
- 1/2 tbsp butter (7g)
- 1 garlic clove, minced (5g)
- 1/4 tsp salt (1g)
- Pinch of thyme (0.25g)
- Pinch black pepper (0.25g)
- Chopped parsley for garnish (optional)

Instructions:

1. Cook wild rice in boiling water (2.5:1 ratio) for 25–30 minutes until tender.
2. Heat butter and olive oil in a pan. Sauté mushrooms with garlic, thyme, salt, and pepper for 6–8 minutes until browned.
3. Poach the egg in simmering water for 3–4 minutes.
4. Combine wild rice with sautéed mushrooms.
5. Top with poached egg and garnish with parsley if desired.

Nutritional Facts (Per Serving): Calories: 478 | Carbs: 34g | Protein: 17g | Fat: 29g | Fiber: 5g | Sodium: 310mg | Sugars: 3g

CHAPTER 8: LUNCH: Hearty Mediterranean Plates

RATATOUILLE WITH WHITE BEANS AND HERBS DE PROVENCE

DIFFICULTY LEVEL: ★★☆ (MODERATE) | PREP: 10 MIN | COOK: 25 MIN | SERVES: 1

Ingredients

- 120g (4.2 oz) canned white beans, drained and rinsed
- 80g (2.8 oz) eggplant, cubed
- 60g (2.1 oz) zucchini, sliced
- 60g (2.1 oz) red bell pepper, chopped
- 40g (1.4 oz) onion, diced
- 1 medium tomato, chopped (100g)
- 1.5 tbsp olive oil (22ml)
- 1/2 tsp Herbs de Provence (1g)
- 1/4 tsp salt (1g)
- 1 garlic clove, minced (5g)
- Pinch black pepper (0.25g)
- Fresh basil or parsley to garnish (optional)

Nutritional Facts (Per Serving): Calories: 486 | Carbs: 44g | Protein: 16g | Fat: 27g | Fiber: 12g | Sodium: 420mg | Sugars: 10g

Instructions:

1. Heat olive oil in a large skillet over medium heat. Add onion and garlic, sauté 3–4 minutes.
2. Add eggplant, zucchini, and bell pepper. Cook 8–1 minutes, stirring occasionally.
3. Stir in tomato, white beans, salt, pepper, and Herb de Provence.
4. Cover and simmer for 10 minutes until vegetable are soft and flavors meld.
5. Serve warm, garnished with herbs if desired.

LEMON-HERB CHICKEN THIGHS WITH COUSCOUS

DIFFICULTY LEVEL: ★★☆ (MODERATE) | PREP: 10 MIN | COOK: 20 MIN | SERVES: 1

Ingredients

- 150g (5.3 oz) boneless skinless chicken thighs
- 60g (2.1 oz) dry couscous
- 1 tbsp olive oil (15ml)
- 1 tbsp lemon juice (15ml)
- 1/2 tsp lemon zest (1g)
- 1/4 tsp dried oregano (0.5g)
- 1 garlic clove, minced (5g)
- 1/4 tsp salt (1g)
- Pinch of black pepper (0.25)
- Fresh parsley for garnish (optional)

Nutritional Facts (Per Serving): Calories: 499 | Carbs: 28g | Protein: 35g | Fat: 27g | Fiber: 2g | Sodium: 390mg | Sugars: 1g

Instructions:

1. Marinate chicken in lemon juice, zest, garli oregano, salt, and pepper for 10 minutes.
2. Heat olive oil in a skillet over medium heat. Coc chicken 5–6 minutes per side until golden and cooke through. Prepare couscous by pouring boiling wat over it (1:1.5 ratio), cover and steam 5 minutes, the fluff with fork.
3. Serve chicken over couscous, garnish with parsley desired.

ZUCCHINI BOATS STUFFED WITH GROUND TURKEY & FARRO

DIFFICULTY LEVEL: ★★☆ (MODERATE) | PREP: 15 MIN | COOK: 30 MIN | SERVES: 1

Ingredients

- 2 small zucchini, halved (200g total)
- 120g (4.2 oz) ground turkey (93% lean)
- 50g (1.8 oz) cooked farro (or 25g dry)
- 1/2 small onion, diced (40g)
- 1 garlic clove, minced (5g)
- 1 tbsp olive oil (15ml)
- 1 tbsp grated parmesan (8g)
- 1/4 tsp dried oregano (0.5g)
- 1/4 tsp salt (1g)
- Pinch of black pepper (0.25g)

Instructions:

1. Cook farro according to package (if using dry) and set aside.
2. Scoop out zucchini halves to create boats. Reserve some flesh and chop.
3. Sauté onion and garlic in olive oil for 3 minutes, add turkey, chopped zucchini flesh, oregano, salt, and pepper. Cook 7–8 minutes.
4. Mix in cooked farro and parmesan.
5. Fill zucchini boats, place in baking dish, cover with foil, and bake at 190°C (375°F) for 20–25 minutes.
6. Serve warm.

Nutritional Facts (Per Serving): Calories: 503 | Carbs: 33g | Protein: 33g | Fat: 26g | Fiber: 6g | Sodium: 380mg | Sugars: 5g

ROASTED BELL PEPPER & CHICKPEA BOWL WITH CUMIN YOGURT

DIFFICULTY LEVEL: ★☆☆ (EASY) | PREP: 10 MIN | COOK: 20 MIN | SERVES: 1

Ingredients

- 120g (4.2 oz) cooked chickpeas
- 1 red bell pepper, sliced (100g)
- 1/2 red onion, sliced (40g)
- 1 tbsp olive oil (15ml)
- 1 tbsp chopped parsley (3g)
- For sauce:
- 100g (3.5 oz) plain Greek yogurt (2% fat)
- 1/2 tsp ground cumin (1g)
- 1/2 tbsp lemon juice (7ml)
- Pinch salt (0.5g)
- 1/2 garlic clove, grated (2g)

Instructions:

1. Toss bell pepper and onion in olive oil and roast at 200°C (400°F) for 20 minutes until tender and slightly charred.
2. Warm chickpeas in a skillet or microwave.
3. Mix yogurt with cumin, lemon juice, garlic, and salt to make the sauce. Combine chickpeas, roasted vegetables, and parsley in a bowl.
4. Drizzle with cumin yogurt and serve.
5. Carefully roll the lettuce leaves into wraps, tucking in the sides to keep the filling secure.
6. Slice each wrap in half and serve immediately.

Nutritional Facts (Per Serving): Calories: 514 | Carbs: 36g | Protein: 19g | Fat: 30g | Fiber: 9g | Sodium: 430mg | Sugars: 7g

COD FILLET WITH GREEN BEANS AND GARLIC-MASHED POTATO

Nutritional Facts (Per Serving): Calories: 487 | Carbs: 32g | Protein: 36g | Fat: 24g | Fiber: 5g | Sodium: 370mg | Sugars: 3g

DIFFICULTY LEVEL: ★★☆ (MODERATE) | PREP: 10 MIN | COOK: 20 MIN | SERVES: 1

Ingredients

- 140g (5 oz) cod fillet
- 100g (3.5 oz) green beans, trimmed
- 120g (4.2 oz) potato, peeled and cubed
- 1 garlic clove (5g)
- 1 tbsp olive oil (15ml)
- 1/2 tbsp unsalted butter (7g)
- 1 tbsp milk (15ml)
- 1/4 tsp salt (1g)
- Pinch black pepper (0.25g)
- Fresh parsley for garnish (optional)

Instructions:

1. Boil potatoes in salted water for 15 minutes until tender. Drain and mash with butter, milk, salt, and garlic.
2. Steam green beans for 4–5 minutes until crisp-tender.
3. Season cod with salt and pepper. Pan-sear in olive oil for 3–4 minutes per side or bake at 200°C (400°F) for 12–14 minutes.
4. Plate cod with mashed potatoes and green beans. Garnish with parsley if desired.

LENTIL STEW WITH CARROTS, CELERY, AND OLIVE OIL DRIZZLE

Nutritional Facts (Per Serving): Calories: 489 | Carbs: 41g | Protein: 21g | Fat: 24g | Fiber: 15g | Sodium: 390mg | Sugars: 7g

DIFFICULTY LEVEL: ★★☆ (MODERATE) | PREP: 10 MIN | COOK: 30 MIN | SERVES: 1

Ingredients

- 75g (2.6 oz) dry green lentils
- 80g (2.8 oz) carrot, diced
- 60g (2.1 oz) celery, sliced
- 40g (1.4 oz) onion, chopped
- 1 garlic clove, minced (5g)
- 1 tbsp olive oil (15ml)
- 1/2 tbsp olive oil for drizzle (7ml)
- 1/4 tsp dried thyme (0.5g)
- 1/4 tsp salt (1g)
- Pinch black pepper (0.25g)
- 500ml water (for cooking)

Instructions:

1. Rinse lentils and cook in a pot with 500ml water, simmering for 25–30 minutes until tender.
2. Meanwhile, in a skillet, heat 1 tbsp olive oil. Sauté onion, garlic, carrots, and celery with thyme, salt, and pepper for 8–10 minutes.
3. Combine cooked lentils with sautéed vegetables. Simmer together for 5 minutes.
4. Serve warm, drizzled with remaining olive oil.

EGGPLANT & TOMATO BAKE WITH BASIL RICOTTA

DIFFICULTY LEVEL: ★★☆ (MODERATE) | PREP: 15 MIN | COOK: 30 MIN | SERVES: 1

Ingredients

- 120g (4.2 oz) eggplant, sliced
- 100g (3.5 oz) tomatoes, sliced
- 80g (2.8 oz) ricotta cheese
- 1 tbsp grated parmesan (8g)
- 1 tbsp olive oil (15ml)
- 1 garlic clove, minced (5g)
- 1 tbsp chopped fresh basil (3g)
- 1/4 tsp salt (1g)
- Pinch black pepper (0.25g)

Instructions:

1. Brush eggplant slices with olive oil and roast at 200°C (400°F) for 15–20 minutes until tender.
2. In a bowl, mix ricotta with basil, garlic, salt, and pepper.
3. In a small baking dish, layer roasted eggplant, sliced tomato, and ricotta mixture.
4. Top with parmesan and bake uncovered for 10 minutes until bubbly.
5. Serve hot or warm.

Nutritional Facts (Per Serving): Calories: 478 | Carbs: 23g | Protein: 20g | Fat: 33g | Fiber: 6g | Sodium: 370mg | Sugars: 9g

GRILLED SHRIMP WITH BULGUR-PARSLEY SALAD

DIFFICULTY LEVEL: ★★☆ (MODERATE) | PREP: 15 MIN | COOK: 10 MIN | SERVES: 1

Ingredients

- 120g (4.2 oz) raw shrimp, peeled
- 60g (2.1 oz) dry bulgur
- 1 tbsp olive oil (15ml)
- 1 tbsp lemon juice (15ml)
- 1 tbsp chopped fresh parsley (3g)
- 1/2 small cucumber, diced (50g)
- 30g (1 oz) cherry tomatoes, halved
- 1 garlic clove, minced (5g)
- 1/4 tsp salt (1g)
- Pinch black pepper (0.25g)

Instructions:

1. Cook bulgur in boiling water (2:1 ratio) for 10–12 minutes. Let cool slightly.
2. Season shrimp with salt, pepper, and garlic. Grill or sauté 2–3 minutes per side.
3. In a bowl, combine cooked bulgur, parsley, cucumber, and tomatoes.
4. Drizzle with olive oil and lemon juice.
5. Top with grilled shrimp and serve warm or chilled.

Nutritional Facts (Per Serving): Calories: 472 | Carbs: 34g | Protein: 27g | Fat: 25g | Fiber: 5g | Sodium: 410mg | Sugars: 2g

CHAPTER 9: LUNCH: Plant-Based Comforts

CANNELLINI BEAN STEW WITH SPINACH AND TOMATOES

Nutritional Facts (Per Serving): Calories: 472 | Carbs: 40g | Protein: 20g | Fat: 24g | Fiber: 10g | Sodium: 410mg | Sugars: 6g

DIFFICULTY LEVEL: ★☆☆ (EASY) | PREP: 10 MIN | COOK: 20 MIN | SERVES: 1

Ingredients

- 140g (5 oz) canned cannellini beans, rinsed and drained
- 80g (2.8 oz) fresh spinach, chopped
- 100g (3.5 oz) chopped tomatoes (canned or fresh)
- 1/2 small onion, chopped (40g)
- 1 garlic clove, minced (5g)
- 1 tbsp olive oil (15ml)
- 1/4 tsp dried thyme (0.5g)
- 1/4 tsp salt (1g)
- Pinch of black pepper (0.25g)

Instructions:

1. Heat olive oil in a saucepan. Sauté onion and garlic for 3–4 minutes until soft.
2. Add tomatoes, thyme, salt, and pepper. Simmer minutes.
3. Stir in cannellini beans and spinach. Simmer for 1 minutes until heated through and spinach is wilted.
4. Serve hot with extra herbs or lemon if desired.

WARM FARRO & VEGETABLE BOWL WITH POACHED EGG

Nutritional Facts (Per Serving): Calories: 494 | Carbs: 37g | Protein: 19g | Fat: 27g | Fiber: 7g | Sodium: 370mg | Sugars: 5g

DIFFICULTY LEVEL: ★★☆ (MODERATE) | PREP: 10 MIN | COOK: 25 MIN | SERVES: 1

Ingredients

- 60g (2.1 oz) dry farro
- 1/2 medium zucchini, chopped (60g)
- 50g (1.8 oz) red bell pepper, chopped
- 1 small carrot, grated (50g)
- 1 garlic clove, minced (5g)
- 1 tbsp olive oil (15ml)
- 1 large egg (50g)
- 1/4 tsp salt (1g)
- Pinch black pepper (0.25g)
- Fresh parsley for garnish (optional)

Instructions:

1. Cook farro in boiling water for 20–25 minutes until tender.
2. In a skillet, heat olive oil and sauté zucchini, carrot, bell pepper, and garlic for 7–8 minutes. Season with salt and pepper.
3. Poach egg in simmering water for 3–4 minutes.
4. Combine cooked farro with vegetables.
5. Top with poached egg and garnish with herbs desired.

ROASTED PUMPKIN WITH LENTILS AND SPICED YOGURT

Nutritional Facts (Per Serving): Calories: 481 | Carbs: 38g | Protein: 19g | Fat: 27g | Fiber: 9g | Sodium: 430mg | Sugars: 10g

DIFFICULTY LEVEL: ★★☆ (MODERATE) | PREP: 10 MIN | COOK: 25 MIN | SERVES: 1

Ingredients

- 140g (5 oz) pumpkin, peeled and cubed
- 60g (2.1 oz) dry green or brown lentils
- 1/2 tbsp olive oil (7ml)
- 1/2 tsp ground cumin (1g)
- 1/4 tsp cinnamon (0.5g)
- 1/4 tsp salt (1g)
- For the yogurt sauce:
- 2 tbsp plain Greek yogurt (40g)
- 1/2 garlic clove, grated (2g)
- 1/2 tbsp lemon juice (7ml)
- 1 tsp olive oil (5ml)
- Pinch salt (0.25g)
- Pinch black pepper (0.25g)

Instructions:

1. Toss pumpkin with olive oil, cumin, cinnamon, salt, and pepper. Roast at 200°C (400°F) for 20–25 minutes until golden.
2. Cook lentils in water for 20–25 minutes until tender.
3. Mix yogurt with garlic, lemon juice, olive oil, and salt to make the sauce.
4. Serve roasted pumpkin with lentils and drizzle with spiced yogurt sauce

BAKED FALAFEL BOWL WITH QUINOA AND LEMON-HERB SAUCE

Nutritional Facts (Per Serving): Calories: 493 | Carbs: 39g | Protein: 19g | Fat: 28g | Fiber: 9g | Sodium: 420mg | Sugars: 4g

DIFFICULTY LEVEL: ★★☆ (MODERATE) | PREP: 15 MIN | COOK: 25 MIN | SERVES: 1

Ingredients

- For the falafel:
- 100g (3.5 oz) cooked chickpeas
- 1 garlic clove, minced (5g)
- 1/4 small onion, chopped (20g)
- 1 tbsp chopped parsley (3g)
- 1 tbsp oat flour or ground oats (8g)
- 1/2 tbsp lemon juice (7ml)
- 1 tsp olive oil (5ml)
- 1 tsp chopped fresh dill or parsley (1g)
- Pinch salt (0.25g)
- 1/2 tbsp olive oil (7ml)
- 1/4 tsp cumin (0.5g)
- 1/4 tsp salt (1g)
- Pinch black pepper (0.25g)
- For the bowl:
- 60g (2.1 oz) dry quinoa
- 50g (1.8 oz) cucumber, diced
- 40g (1.4 oz) cherry tomatoes, halved
- For the sauce:
- 2 tbsp plain Greek yogurt (40g)

Instructions:

1. Preheat oven to 200°C (400°F). Mash chickpeas and combine with onion, garlic, parsley, oat flour, olive oil, cumin, salt, and pepper. Form 3–4 small patties, place on parchment, and bake 20 minutes, flipping once.
4. Cook quinoa in double water for 15 minutes until fluffy. Mix yogurt, lemon juice, olive oil, herbs, and salt to make sauce.
5. Assemble bowl with quinoa, veggies, falafel, and drizzle with sauce.

STUFFED TOMATOES WITH BROWN RICE AND HERBS

Nutritional Facts (Per Serving): Calories: 454 | Carbs: 44g | Protein: 12g | Fat: 26g | Fiber: 6g | Sodium: 370mg | Sugars: 7g

DIFFICULTY LEVEL: ★★☆ (MODERATE) | PREP: 15 MIN | COOK: 25 MIN | SERVES: 1

Ingredients

- 2 large tomatoes (total 300g), tops cut and insides scooped
- 60g (2.1 oz) cooked brown rice
- 20g (0.7 oz) feta cheese, crumbled
- 1 tbsp chopped parsley (3g)
- 1 tbsp chopped fresh basil (3g)
- 1/2 garlic clove, minced (2g)
- 1 tbsp olive oil (15ml)
- 1/4 tsp salt (1g)
- Pinch black pepper (0.25g)

Instructions:

1. Preheat oven to 190°C (375°F).
2. In a bowl, combine cooked rice, feta, parsley, basil, garlic, olive oil, salt, and pepper.
3. Fill hollowed tomatoes with the mixture. Place in a baking dish.
4. Bake uncovered for 20–25 minutes until tomatoes are soft and tops are golden.
5. Serve warm with fresh herbs if desired.

CAULIFLOWER & PEA CURRY WITH WHOLE GRAIN RICE

Nutritional Facts (Per Serving): Calories: 489 | Carbs: 48g | Protein: 13g | Fat: 27g | Fiber: 10g | Sodium: 420mg | Sugars: 7g

DIFFICULTY LEVEL: ★★☆ (MODERATE) | PREP: 10 MIN | COOK: 25 MIN | SERVES: 1

Ingredients

- 100g (3.5 oz) cauliflower florets
- 60g (2.1 oz) green peas (frozen or fresh)
- 1/2 small onion, chopped (40g)
- 1 garlic clove, minced (5g)
- 1/2 tsp grated ginger (2g)
- 1/2 tsp curry powder (1g)
- 1/4 tsp ground turmeric (0.5g)
- 1 tbsp olive oil (15ml)
- 1/4 cup canned coconut milk (60ml)
- 1/4 tsp salt (1g)
- Pinch black pepper (0.25g)
- For the side:
- 60g (2.1 oz) cooked whole grain rice

Instructions:

1. Heat olive oil in a pan and sauté onion, garlic, and ginger for 3 minutes.
2. Add cauliflower and peas, cook 5 minutes.
3. Stir in curry powder, turmeric, salt, and pepper.
4. Pour in coconut milk, cover and simmer 10–12 minutes until vegetables are tender.
5. Serve with cooked whole grain rice.

CHICKPEA PATTIES WITH CARROT SLAW AND YOGURT DIP

DIFFICULTY LEVEL: ★★☆ (MODERATE) | **PREP:** 15 MIN | **COOK:** 15 MIN | **SERVES:** 1

Ingredients

- For the patties:
- 100g (3.5 oz) cooked chickpeas
- 1 tbsp oat flour (8g)
- 1 garlic clove, minced (5g)
- 1 tbsp chopped parsley (3g)
- 1/4 small onion, finely chopped (20g)
- 1/2 tbsp olive oil (7ml)
- 1/4 tsp salt (1g)
- Pinch black pepper (0.25g)
- For the slaw:
- 60g (2.1 oz) grated carrot
- 1 tsp lemon juice (5ml)
- 1 tsp olive oil (5ml)
- For the dip:
- 2 tbsp plain Greek yogurt (40g)
- 1/2 garlic clove, grated (2g)
- Pinch salt (0.25g)

Instructions:

1. Mash chickpeas and mix with oat flour, onion, garlic, parsley, olive oil, salt, and pepper. Form 3 patties.
2. Pan-fry on nonstick skillet 4–5 minutes per side until golden.
3. Mix grated carrot with lemon juice and olive oil.
4. Combine yogurt with garlic and salt for dip.
5. Serve patties with carrot slaw and yogurt dip on the side.

Nutritional Facts (Per Serving): Calories: 477 | Carbs: 38g | Protein: 19g | Fat: 27g | Fiber: 9g | Sodium: 390mg | Sugars: 7g

POLENTA WITH SAUTÉED KALE AND WHITE BEANS

DIFFICULTY LEVEL: ★★☆ (MODERATE) | **PREP:** 10 MIN | **COOK:** 25 MIN | **SERVES:** 1

Ingredients

- 60g (2.1 oz) dry polenta (cornmeal)
- 120ml (1/2 cup) unsweetened plant-based milk or water
- 100g (3.5 oz) canned white beans, rinsed
- 60g (2.1 oz) kale, chopped
- 1 garlic clove, minced (5g)
- 1 tbsp olive oil (15ml)
- 1 tsp lemon juice (5ml)
- 1 tbsp nutritional yeast (7g)
- 1/4 tsp salt (1g)
- Pinch black pepper (0.25g)

Instructions:

1. Cook polenta in milk or water with a pinch of salt, stirring frequently for 10–15 minutes until thick. Stir in nutritional yeast.
2. Sauté garlic and kale in olive oil over medium heat for 4–5 minutes. Add beans and lemon juice, heat through.
3. Plate polenta and top with kale-bean mixture. Serve warm.

Nutritional Facts (Per Serving): Calories: 498 | Carbs: 41g | Protein: 18g | Fat: 28g | Fiber: 8g | Sodium: 400mg | Sugars: 2g

CHAPTER 10: LUNCH: Balanced Protein Mains

GRILLED SALMON WITH BROCCOLI AND LEMON COUSCOUS

DIFFICULTY LEVEL: ★★☆ (MODERATE) | PREP: 10 MIN | COOK: 15 MIN | SERVES: 1

Ingredients

- 130g (4.6 oz) salmon fillet
- 100g (3.5 oz) broccoli florets
- 50g (1.8 oz) dry couscous
- 1 tbsp olive oil (15ml)
- 1 tbsp lemon juice (15ml)
- 1/2 tsp lemon zest (1g)
- 1/4 tsp salt (1g)
- Pinch black pepper (0.25g)

Instructions:

1. Season salmon with salt and pepper. Grill or pan-sear for 3–4 minutes per side until cooked through.
2. Steam broccoli for 4–5 minutes until tender.
3. Cook couscous by pouring boiling water (75ml) over it, cover for 5 minutes, then fluff with fork. Stir in lemon juice, zest, and olive oil.
4. Serve salmon with couscous and broccoli on the side.

Nutritional Facts (Per Serving): Calories: 504 | Carbs: 26g | Protein: 34g | Fat: 31g | Fiber: 4g | Sodium: 370mg | Sugars: 1g

TURKEY & CHICKPEA BOWL WITH OLIVE DRESSING

DIFFICULTY LEVEL: ★★☆ (MODERATE) | PREP: 15 MIN | COOK: 15 MIN | SERVES: 1

Ingredients

- 100g (3.5 oz) ground turkey (93% lean)
- 100g (3.5 oz) cooked chickpeas
- 50g (1.8 oz) cucumber, diced
- 30g (1 oz) cherry tomatoes, halved
- 1 tbsp chopped parsley (3g)
- For the dressing:
- 1 tbsp chopped green olives (15g)
- 1 tbsp olive oil (15ml)
- 1 tsp red wine vinegar (5ml)
- 1/4 tsp mustard (1g)
- 1/4 tsp salt (1g)
- Pinch black pepper (0.25g)

Instructions:

1. Cook ground turkey in a nonstick pan over medium heat until fully cooked, about 7–8 minutes. Season lightly.
2. Mix chickpeas, cucumber, tomatoes, and parsley in a bowl.
3. For dressing, whisk together olive oil, olives, vinegar, mustard, salt, and pepper.
4. Assemble bowl: place turkey and chickpea salad, drizzle with olive dressing.

Nutritional Facts (Per Serving): Calories: 495 | Carbs: 28g | Protein: 35g | Fat: 27g | Fiber: 6g | Sodium: 420mg | Sugars: 3g

BAKED WHITE FISH WITH LENTILS AND TOMATO SALSA

DIFFICULTY LEVEL: ★★☆ (MODERATE) | **PREP:** 10 MIN | **COOK:** 25 MIN | **SERVES:** 1

Ingredients

- 130g (4.6 oz) white fish fillet (e.g. cod or haddock)
- 60g (2.1 oz) dry green lentils
- 1/2 tbsp olive oil (7ml)
- 1/4 tsp salt (1g)
- Pinch black pepper (0.25g)
- For the salsa:
- 80g (2.8 oz) tomatoes, diced
- 1 tbsp red onion, minced (10g)
- 1 tsp olive oil (5ml)
- 1/2 tbsp lemon juice (7ml)
- 1 tbsp parsley or cilantro (3g)
- Pinch salt (0.25g)

Instructions:

1. Season fish with salt and pepper, brush with olive oil, and bake at 200°C (400°F) for 15–18 minutes.
2. Cook lentils in water for 20–25 minutes until tender.
3. Mix salsa ingredients: tomatoes, onion, oil, lemon juice, and herbs.
4. Plate lentils, top with fish and salsa.

Nutritional Facts (Per Serving): Calories: 471 | Carbs: 27g | Protein: 36g | Fat: 25g | Fiber: 6g | Sodium: 390mg | Sugars: 5g

CHICKEN & EGGPLANT SAUTÉ WITH COUSCOUS

DIFFICULTY LEVEL: ★★☆ (MODERATE) | **PREP:** 10 MIN | **COOK:** 20 MIN | **SERVES:** 1

Ingredients

- 130g (4.6 oz) chicken breast, cubed
- 100g (3.5 oz) eggplant, diced
- 50g (1.8 oz) dry couscous
- 1 garlic clove, minced (5g)
- 1/2 tbsp olive oil (7ml)
- 1/2 tbsp lemon juice (7ml)
- 1/4 tsp dried oregano (0.5g)
- 1/4 tsp salt (1g)
- Pinch black pepper (0.25g)

Instructions:

1. Cook couscous with boiling water (75ml), cover and steam 5 minutes, then fluff.
2. Sauté chicken and garlic in olive oil over medium heat until browned and cooked through.
3. Add eggplant, oregano, salt, and pepper. Cook 8–10 minutes until tender.
4. Stir in lemon juice. Serve over couscous.

Nutritional Facts (Per Serving): Calories: 489 | Carbs: 31g | Protein: 36g | Fat: 26g | Fiber: 5g | Sodium: 410mg | Sugars: 6g

SPAGHETTI SQUASH WITH SARDINES AND CAPERS

DIFFICULTY LEVEL: ★★☆ (MODERATE) | PREP: 10 MIN | COOK: 30 MIN | SERVES: 1

Ingredients

- 200g (7 oz) cooked spaghetti squash
- 90g (3.2 oz) canned sardines in olive oil, drained
- 1 tbsp olive oil (15ml)
- 1 tsp capers (5g)
- 1 garlic clove, minced (5g)
- 1 tbsp chopped parsley (3g)
- 1/2 tsp lemon zest (1g)
- 1 tsp lemon juice (5ml)
- 1/4 tsp salt (1g)
- Pinch black pepper (0.25g)

Instructions:

1. Bake spaghetti squash halves at 200°C (400°F) for 25–30 minutes. Scrape strands with fork.
2. In a skillet, heat olive oil and sauté garlic for 1 minute.
3. Add sardines, capers, and squash. Stir gently to combine.
4. Season with salt, pepper, lemon juice, and zest. Top with parsley and serve.

Nutritional Facts (Per Serving): Calories: 483 | Carbs: 19g | Protein: 26g | Fat: 34g | Fiber: 5g | Sodium: 420mg | Sugars: 7g

ZUCCHINI-LENTIL CAKES WITH GARLIC YOGURT

DIFFICULTY LEVEL: ★★☆ (MODERATE) | PREP: 15 MIN | COOK: 15 MIN | SERVES: 1

Ingredients

- 80g (2.8 oz) zucchini, grated
- 70g (2.5 oz) cooked lentils
- 1 egg (50g)
- 1 tbsp oat flour (8g)
- 1/2 garlic clove, minced (2g)
- 1 tbsp chopped parsley (3g)
- 1 tbsp olive oil (15ml)

- For the sauce:
- 2 tbsp plain Greek yogurt (40g)
- 1/2 garlic clove, grated (2g)
- 1 tsp lemon juice (5ml)
- Pinch salt (0.25g)

Instructions:

1. Grate zucchini and squeeze excess moisture.
2. Mix with lentils, egg, oat flour, garlic, parsley, and form patties.
3. Heat olive oil in skillet and pan-fry cakes 3–4 minutes per side.
4. Mix yogurt with garlic, lemon juice, and salt.
5. Serve cakes with garlic yogurt on the side.

Nutritional Facts (Per Serving): Calories: 497 | Carbs: 33g | Protein: 21g | Fat: 30g | Fiber: 6g | Sodium: 400mg | Sugars: 6g

SHRIMP & BELL PEPPER STIR-FRY WITH BARLEY (WITH OLIVE OIL BOOST)

Nutritional Facts (Per Serving): Calories: 508 | Carbs: 35g | Protein: 29g | Fat: 28g | Fiber: 6g | Sodium: 410mg | Sugars: 4g

DIFFICULTY LEVEL: ★★☆ (MODERATE) | PREP: 10 MIN | COOK: 20 MIN | SERVES: 1

Ingredients

- 120g (4.2 oz) raw shrimp, peeled
- 60g (2.1 oz) red bell pepper, sliced
- 40g (1.4 oz) yellow bell pepper, sliced
- 1 garlic clove, minced (5g)
- 60g (2.1 oz) cooked barley
- 1 tbsp olive oil (15ml)
- 1 tsp extra olive oil boost (5ml)
- 1/4 tsp paprika (0.5g)
- 1/4 tsp salt (1g)
- Pinch chili flakes (optional)

Instructions:

1. Cook barley in water if not pre-cooked.
2. Sauté garlic in olive oil. Add shrimp and cook 2–3 minutes per side.
3. Add bell peppers, salt, paprika, chili flakes. Stir-fry until tender-crisp.
4. Stir in barley, drizzle with extra olive oil, serve warm.

SAUTÉED MUSHROOMS AND BEANS WITH POACHED EGG

Nutritional Facts (Per Serving): Calories: 479 | Carbs: 28g | Protein: 21g | Fat: 30g | Fiber: 8g | Sodium: 380mg | Sugars: 4g

DIFFICULTY LEVEL: ★★☆ (EASY) | PREP: 10 MIN | COOK: 15 MIN | SERVES: 1

Ingredients

- 100g (3.5 oz) mushrooms, sliced
- 100g (3.5 oz) canned white beans, rinsed
- 1 large egg (50g)
- 1 garlic clove, minced (5g)
- 1 tbsp olive oil (15ml)
- 1 tsp balsamic vinegar (5ml)
- 1 tbsp chopped parsley (3g)
- 1/4 tsp salt (1g)
- Pinch black pepper (0.25g)

Instructions:

1. Sauté mushrooms and garlic in olive oil over medium heat until golden.
2. Add beans, salt, pepper, and balsamic vinegar. Cook 3–4 minutes.
3. Poach the egg in simmering water for 3–4 minutes.
4. Serve mushroom-bean mix topped with poached egg and parsley.

CHAPTER 11: SNACK: With a spoon and with pleasure

RICOTTA CREAM WITH STEWED PEACHES AND CINNAMON

DIFFICULTY LEVEL: ★☆☆ (EASY) | PREP: 5 MIN | COOK: 5 MIN | SERVES: 1

Ingredients

- 80g (2.8 oz) whole milk ricotta
- 1 medium peach, sliced (100g)
- 1/2 tsp honey (3g)
- 1/4 tsp ground cinnamon (0.5g)
- 1 tsp water (5ml)

Instructions:

1. In a small pan, simmer sliced peach with water and cinnamon over low heat for 4–5 minutes until soft.
2. In a bowl, whip ricotta until smooth.
3. Top ricotta with stewed peaches and drizzle with honey. Serve warm or chilled.

Nutritional Facts (Per Serving): Calories: 197 | Carbs: 13g | Protein: 9g | Fat: 12g | Fiber: 1g | Sodium: 60mg | Sugars: 11g

CHIA PUDDING WITH BAKED BERRIES AND VANILLA

DIFFICULTY LEVEL: ★☆☆ (EASY) | PREP: 5 MIN (+ chill) | COOK: 10 MIN | SERVES: 1

Ingredients

- 2 tbsp chia seeds (20g)
- 120ml (1/2 cup) unsweetened almond milk
- 1/2 tsp vanilla extract (2ml)
- 60g (2.1 oz) mixed berries (fresh or frozen)
- 1/2 tsp honey (3g)

Instructions:

1. Mix chia seeds, almond milk, and vanilla in a small jar. Chill for 3+ hours or overnight.
2. Bake berries at 180°C (350°F) for 10 minutes until soft.
3. Top pudding with warm baked berries and drizzle with honey.

Nutritional Facts (Per Serving): Calories: 198 | Carbs: 14g | Protein: 6g | Fat: 12g | Fiber: 6g | Sodium: 35mg | Sugars: 7g

COTTAGE CHEESE MOUSSE WITH GRATED APPLE AND NUTMEG

DIFFICULTY LEVEL: ★☆☆ (EASY) | PREP: 5 MIN | COOK: 0 MIN | SERVES: 1

Ingredients

- 100g (3.5 oz) low-fat cottage cheese (2% fat)
- 1/2 medium apple, grated (75g)
- 1/2 tsp honey (3g)
- 1/8 tsp ground nutmeg (0.25g)

Instructions:

1. Blend cottage cheese until smooth.
2. Mix in grated apple, honey, and a pinch of nutmeg.
3. Serve immediately or chilled.

Nutritional Facts (Per Serving): Calories: 194 | Carbs: 14g | Protein: 14g | Fat: 9g | Fiber: 1g | Sodium: 160mg | Sugars: 11g

YOGURT & PUMPKIN PURÉE WITH CLOVE AND ORANGE ZEST

DIFFICULTY LEVEL: ★☆☆ (EASY) | PREP: 5 MIN | COOK: 5 MIN | SERVES: 1

Ingredients

- 100g (3.5 oz) plain Greek yogurt (2%)
- 60g (2.1 oz) pumpkin purée (unsweetened)
- 1/2 tsp honey (3g)
- 1/4 tsp orange zest (1g)
- 1/8 tsp ground cloves (0.25g)

Instructions:

1. Gently heat pumpkin purée with cloves and honey for 2–3 minutes until warm.
2. Stir in orange zest.
3. Layer warm pumpkin over yogurt or swirl together. Serve immediately.

Nutritional Facts (Per Serving): Calories: 196 | Carbs: 15g | Protein: 10g | Fat: 10g | Fiber: 2g | Sodium: 55mg | Sugars: 8g

PEAR COMPOTE WITH YOGURT AND SESAME CRUMBLE

DIFFICULTY LEVEL: ★★☆ (EASY) | PREP: 5 MIN | COOK: 8 MIN | SERVES: 1

Ingredients

- 1 small pear, diced (100g)
- 1/2 tsp honey (3g)
- 1/4 tsp cinnamon (0.5g)
- 1/2 tsp lemon juice (2ml)
- For serving:
- 80g (2.8 oz) plain Greek yogurt (2%)
- 1 tsp sesame seeds (3g)
- 1/2 tsp rolled oats (2g)

Instructions:

1. In a pan, simmer pear with honey, lemon juice, and cinnamon for 6–8 minutes until soft.
2. Lightly toast sesame seeds and oats in a dry skillet until golden (1–2 minutes).
3. Layer yogurt with warm pear compote and top with sesame crumble.

Nutritional Facts (Per Serving): Calories: 198 | Carbs: 20g | Protein: 7g | Fat: 10g | Fiber: 2g | Sodium: 40mg | Sugars: 15g

MASHED BANANA CUSTARD WITH LEMON AND CARDAMOM

DIFFICULTY LEVEL: ★★☆ (EASY) | PREP: 5 MIN | COOK: 5 MIN | SERVES: 1

Ingredients

- 1/2 medium ripe banana, mashed (60g)
- 1/2 tsp lemon juice (2ml)
- 1/8 tsp ground cardamom (0.25g)
- 100ml unsweetened plant milk (almond or oat)
- 1 tsp cornstarch (3g)
- 1/2 tsp honey (3g)

Instructions:

1. In a small saucepan, whisk milk with cornstarch. Heat gently until it begins to thicken.
2. Stir in mashed banana, lemon juice, honey, and cardamom. Cook 1–2 minutes more, stirring.
3. Transfer to a dish and chill or serve warm.

Nutritional Facts (Per Serving): Calories: 201 | Carbs: 24g | Protein: 6g | Fat: 9g | Fiber: 2g | Sodium: 45mg | Sugars: 14g

WARM QUINOA DESSERT WITH DATE SYRUP AND COCONUT MILK

DIFFICULTY LEVEL: ★★☆ (MODERATE) | PREP: 5 MIN | COOK: 15 MIN | SERVES: 1

Ingredients

- 40g (1.4 oz) cooked quinoa
- 60ml (1/4 cup) light coconut milk
- 1 tsp date syrup (7g)
- 1/4 tsp vanilla extract (1ml)
- 1/2 tsp shredded coconut (2g)

Instructions:

1. In a small pan, warm quinoa with coconut milk and vanilla over low heat for 5–6 minutes.
2. Transfer to a bowl, drizzle with date syrup and top with shredded coconut. Serve warm.

Nutritional Facts (Per Serving): Calories: 199 | Carbs: 22g | Protein: 5g | Fat: 10g | Fiber: 2g | Sodium: 30mg | Sugars: 10g

CREAMY CARROT PUDDING WITH RAISINS AND CINNAMON

DIFFICULTY LEVEL: ★★☆ (MODERATE) | PREP: 10 MIN | COOK: 15 MIN | SERVES: 1

Ingredients

- 80g (2.8 oz) grated carrot
- 1 tsp raisins (5g)
- 100ml plant-based milk (almond or oat)
- 1 tsp honey (3g)
- 1/4 tsp ground cinnamon (0.5g)
- 1 tsp cornstarch (3g)

Instructions:

1. In a pan, cook grated carrot in milk with raisins and cinnamon over medium heat for 10 minutes.
2. Stir in cornstarch and honey, cook 2–3 minutes more until thickened.
3. Serve warm or chilled.

Nutritional Facts (Per Serving): Calories: 202 | Carbs: 23g | Protein: 5g | Fat: 10g | Fiber: 2g | Sodium: 60mg | Sugars: 14g

CHAPTER 12: SNACK: Baked Delights

HONEY-RICOTTA APPLE BOATS WITH TOASTED ALMOND DUST

Nutritional Facts (Per Serving): Calories: 198 | Carbs: 23g | Protein: 7g | Fat: 9g | Fiber: 3g | Sodium: 55mg | Sugars: 18g

DIFFICULTY LEVEL: ★☆☆ (EASY) | **PREP:** 10 MIN | **COOK:** 20 MIN | **SERVES:** 1

Ingredients

- 1 small apple, halved and cored (120g)
- 60g ricotta cheese (1/4 cup)
- 1 tsp honey (7g)
- 1/2 tsp lemon juice (2.5ml)
- 1/2 tbsp sliced almonds (5g)
- 1/4 tsp ground cinnamon (0.5g)

Instructions:

1. Preheat oven to 180°C (350°F).
2. Place apple halves in a small baking dish, drizzle with lemon juice and bake for 15–18 minutes until tender.
3. Meanwhile, toast sliced almonds in a dry pan over low heat for 2–3 minutes until golden.
4. Remove apples from oven and let cool slightly. Fill the center of each half with ricotta, drizzle with honey and sprinkle with cinnamon and toasted almonds.
5. Serve warm or at room temperature.

BALSAMIC-GLAZED FIGS WITH CREAMY YOGURT CLOUDS

Nutritional Facts (Per Serving): Calories: 194 | Carbs: 20g | Protein: 6g | Fat: 9g | Fiber: 3g | Sodium: 45mg | Sugars: 17g

DIFFICULTY LEVEL: ★☆☆ (EASY) | **PREP:** 10 MIN | **COOK:** 10 MIN | **SERVES:** 1

Ingredients

- 3 fresh figs, halved (120g)
- 80g plain Greek yogurt (about 1/3 cup)
- 1 tsp balsamic glaze (5ml)
- 1/2 tsp honey (3g)
- 1/4 tsp vanilla extract (1ml)
- 1/2 tsp olive oil (2.5ml)
- Pinch of sea salt

Instructions:

1. Preheat oven to 200°C (390°F). Arrange fig halves cut side up in a small baking dish. Drizzle with balsamic glaze and a few drops of olive oil.
2. Roast for 8–10 minutes, until tender and lightly caramelized.
3. While figs roast, mix Greek yogurt with vanilla extract, honey, and a pinch of salt.
4. Serve figs warm, spooned over or beside chilled yogurt clouds. Garnish with an extra drop of glaze if desired.

VELVETY PUMPKIN YOGURT BOWL WITH POMEGRANATE JEWELS

DIFFICULTY LEVEL: ★☆☆ (EASY) | **PREP:** 10 MIN | **COOK:** 10 MIN | **SERVES:** 1

Ingredients

- 1/2 cup pumpkin purée (120g)
- 80g plain Greek yogurt (about 1/3 cup)
- 1 tbsp pomegranate seeds (10g)
- 1 tsp maple syrup or honey (7g)
- 1/4 tsp cinnamon (0.5g)
- 1/8 tsp ground ginger (0.25g)
- 1/4 tsp orange zest (1g)

Instructions:

1. In a small saucepan, gently warm the pumpkin purée with cinnamon and ginger over low heat for 4–5 minutes, stirring occasionally.
2. Remove from heat and let cool slightly.
3. Mix yogurt with orange zest and maple syrup.
4. Layer warm pumpkin at the base of a bowl and spoon the yogurt mixture over it.
5. Top with pomegranate seeds and serve immediately.

Nutritional Facts (Per Serving): Calories: 196 | Carbs: 21g | Protein: 8g | Fat: 8g | Fiber: 3g | Sodium: 50mg | Sugars: 13g

WARM PEAR DELIGHT WITH VANILLA-SCENTED COTTAGE CREAM

DIFFICULTY LEVEL: ★☆☆ (EASY) | **PREP:** 5 MIN | **COOK:** 15 MIN | **SERVES:** 1

Ingredients

- 1 small ripe pear, halved and cored (130g)
- 80g low-fat cottage cheese (about 1/3 cup)
- 1/4 tsp vanilla extract (1ml)
- 1 tsp honey (7g)
- 1/2 tsp olive oil (2.5ml)
- Pinch of cinnamon (optional)

Instructions:

1. Preheat oven to 180°C (350°F). Lightly brush pear halves with olive oil and place in a small baking dish cut side up.
2. Roast for 12–15 minutes, until soft and lightly golden.
3. In the meantime, mix cottage cheese with vanilla extract and half the honey.
4. Place the warm pears on a plate and top with the cottage cream.
5. Drizzle with remaining honey and a touch of cinnamon if desired. Serve immediately.

Nutritional Facts (Per Serving): Calories: 199 | Carbs: 22g | Protein: 10g | Fat: 8g | Fiber: 3g | Sodium: 115mg | Sugars: 17g

ZUCCHINI CITRUS CUSTARD WITH ORANGE ZEST AND OLIVE OIL CRUMBS

Nutritional Facts (Per Serving): Calories: 198 | Carbs: 19g | Protein: 7g | Fat: 11g | Fiber: 2g | Sodium: 60mg | Sugars: 10g

DIFFICULTY LEVEL: ★★☆ (MODERATE) | PREP: 10 MIN | COOK: 20 MIN | SERVES: 1

Ingredients

- 80g grated zucchini (moisture squeezed out)
- 1 medium egg (50g)
- 2 tbsp plain Greek yogurt (30g)
- 1 tsp honey (7g)
- 1/4 tsp orange zest (1g)
- 1/4 tsp vanilla extract (1ml)
- 1/8 tsp ground cinnamon
- 1/2 tbsp olive oil (7ml)
- 1 tbsp oat crumbs or crushed wholegrain biscuit (7g)

Instructions:

1. Preheat oven to 180°C (350°F). Lightly oil a ramekin or small baking dish.
2. In a bowl, whisk together egg, yogurt, honey, vanilla, cinnamon, and orange zest. Stir in grated zucchini.
3. Pour the mixture into the prepared ramekin and bake for 18–20 minutes, until just set in the center.
4. Meanwhile, toast oat crumbs with olive oil in a dry skillet for 2–3 minutes until lightly crisped.
5. Top warm custard with olive oil crumbs before serving.

CINNAMON-STEAM BANANA CAKE WITH DATE SYRUP DRIZZLE

Nutritional Facts (Per Serving): Calories: 200 | Carbs: 27g | Protein: 6g | Fat: 7g | Fiber: 3g | Sodium: 95mg | Sugars: 15g

DIFFICULTY LEVEL: ★★☆ (MODERATE) | PREP: 10 MIN | COOK: 20 MIN (STEAM) | SERVES: 1

Ingredients

- 1 small ripe banana, mashed (100g)
- 1 medium egg (50g)
- 2 tbsp fine semolina (20g)
- 1/2 tsp baking powder (1.5g)
- 1/4 tsp cinnamon (0.5g)
- 1/2 tsp olive oil (2.5ml)
- 1 tsp date syrup or honey (7g)
- Pinch of sea salt

Instructions:

1. In a small bowl, mash the banana and whisk in egg, semolina, baking powder, cinnamon, olive oil, and salt until smooth.
2. Pour mixture into a lightly greased ramekin or small heatproof bowl.
3. Place ramekin in a pot with 1 inch (2.5 cm) of simmering water. Cover pot with lid and steam for 18–20 minutes until set and puffed.
4. Remove carefully and let cool for 2–3 minutes. Drizzle with date syrup before serving.

ROASTED PLUM PARCELS WITH LEMON-RICOTTA HEART

Nutritional Facts (Per Serving): Calories: 193 | Carbs: 19g | Protein: 7g | Fat: 9g | Fiber: 2g | Sodium: 60mg | Sugars: 16g

DIFFICULTY LEVEL: ★☆☆ (EASY) | PREP: 10 MIN | COOK: 15 MIN | SERVES: 1

Ingredients

- 2 ripe plums, halved and pitted (130g)
- 60g ricotta cheese (about 1/4 cup)
- 1/4 tsp lemon zest (1g)
- 1/2 tsp honey (3g)
- 1/2 tsp olive oil (2.5ml)
- Pinch of cinnamon
- Small sprig of fresh thyme (optional)

Instructions:

1. Preheat oven to 190°C (375°F). Place plum halves in a small baking dish, cut side up.
2. In a small bowl, mix ricotta with lemon zest and honey.
3. Spoon a heaping teaspoon of ricotta filling into the center of each plum half.
4. Drizzle plums lightly with olive oil, sprinkle with cinnamon, and add thyme if using.
5. Bake for 12–15 minutes, until plums are soft and the tops are lightly golden. Serve warm.

CARAMELIZED PEACH HALVES WITH SESAME YOGURT SWIRL

Nutritional Facts (Per Serving): Calories: 198 | Carbs: 22g | Protein: 7g | Fat: 9g | Fiber: 3g | Sodium: 55mg | Sugars: 17g

DIFFICULTY LEVEL: ★☆☆ (EASY) | PREP: 5 MIN | COOK: 10 MIN | SERVES: 1

Ingredients

- 1 medium ripe peach, halved and pitted (130g)
- 1/2 tsp olive oil (2.5ml)
- 1/2 tsp honey (3g)
- 2 tbsp plain Greek yogurt (30g)
- 1/2 tsp tahini (3g)
- 1/4 tsp vanilla extract (1ml)
- 1/4 tsp lemon juice (1ml)
- Pinch of toasted sesame seeds (optional)

Instructions:

1. Heat a nonstick skillet over medium heat. Brush peach halves with olive oil and place cut side down.
2. Cook for 4–5 minutes until golden and caramelized. Flip and cook the other side for 2–3 minutes.
3. Meanwhile, stir together Greek yogurt, tahini, vanilla, and lemon juice until smooth.
4. Place warm peach halves in a dish. Top each with the sesame-yogurt swirl and drizzle lightly with honey.
5. Sprinkle with toasted sesame seeds if desired.

CHAPTER 13: Light Creams and Mousses

DATE-BANANA MOUSSE WITH YOGURT AND COCOA

DIFFICULTY LEVEL: ★☆☆ (EASY) | PREP: 5 MIN | CHILL: 15 MIN | SERVES: 1

Ingredients

- 1/2 small banana, mashed (50g)
- 2 soft dates, pitted (30g)
- 80g (2.8 oz) plain Greek yogurt (2%)
- 1/2 tsp unsweetened cocoa powder (1g)
- 1/4 tsp vanilla extract (1ml)

Instructions:

1. Blend banana, dates, yogurt, cocoa, and vanilla until smooth and creamy.
2. Transfer to a serving dish and chill for 10–15 minutes before serving.

Nutritional Facts (Per Serving): Calories: 198 | Carbs: 25g | Protein: 6g | Fat: 7g | Fiber: 3g | Sodium: 40mg | Sugars: 18g

LIGHT FIG CREAM WITH RICOTTA AND MINT

DIFFICULTY LEVEL: ★☆☆ (EASY) | PREP: 5 MIN | SERVES: 1

Ingredients

- 2 medium fresh figs, peeled (70g)
- 40g (1.4 oz) whole milk ricotta
- 1/2 tsp honey (3g)
- 1 fresh mint leaf (optional, 0.3g)

Instructions:

1. Mash or blend figs with ricotta and honey until smooth.
2. Garnish with chopped mint before serving chilled or at room temperature.

Nutritional Facts (Per Serving): Calories: 192 | Carbs: 19g | Protein: 6g | Fat: 9g | Fiber: 3g | Sodium: 50mg | Sugars: 13g

ORANGE-RAISIN SEMOLINA WITH GREEK YOGURT

DIFFICULTY LEVEL: ★★☆ (MODERATE) | **PREP:** 5 MIN | **COOK:** 8 MIN | **SERVES:** 1

Ingredients

- 1 tbsp semolina (10g)
- 80ml unsweetened almond milk
- 1/2 tsp honey (3g)
- 1/2 tsp orange zest (1g)
- 1 tsp raisins (5g)
- 50g (1.8 oz) plain Greek yogurt (2%)

Instructions:

1. Heat almond milk in a saucepan and slowly whisk in semolina.
2. Cook over low heat for 5–6 minutes until thickened. Stir in raisins, zest, and honey.
3. Serve with a dollop of Greek yogurt on top.

Nutritional Facts (Per Serving): Calories: 200 | Carbs: 23g | Protein: 7g | Fat: 8g | Fiber: 2g | Sodium: 60mg | Sugars: 12g

LENTIL-DATE DESSERT PURÉE WITH ROSE WATER

DIFFICULTY LEVEL: ★★☆ (MODERATE) | **PREP:** 10 MIN | **COOK:** 15 MIN | **SERVES:** 1

Ingredients

- 40g (1.4 oz) cooked red lentils
- 2 soft dates, pitted (30g)
- 1 tsp olive oil (5ml)
- 1/2 tsp rose water (2ml)
- 1 tbsp unsweetened almond milk (15ml)

Instructions:

1. Blend all ingredients until smooth.
2. Warm gently in a pan over low heat for 3–4 minutes before serving, or serve chilled.

Nutritional Facts (Per Serving): Calories: 196 | Carbs: 22g | Protein: 7g | Fat: 7g | Fiber: 3g | Sodium: 50mg | Sugars: 11g

APPLE-CINNAMON MILLET CREAM WITH YOGURT

DIFFICULTY LEVEL: ★★☆ (MODERATE) | PREP: 5 MIN | COOK: 15 MIN | SERVES: 1

Ingredients

- 2 tbsp cooked millet (30g)
- 1/2 small apple, grated (60g)
- 50ml unsweetened almond milk
- 1/2 tsp honey (3g)
- 1/4 tsp cinnamon (0.5g)
- 1 tbsp plain Greek yogurt (15g)

Instructions:

1. Heat almond milk with millet and grated apple in a saucepan. Simmer for 8–10 minutes.
2. Stir in honey and cinnamon. Serve warm topped with Greek yogurt.

Nutritional Facts (Per Serving): Calories: 197 | Carbs: 27g | Protein: 5g | Fat: 7g | Fiber: 3g | Sodium: 45mg | Sugars: 12g

GRAPE COMPOTE WITH RICOTTA AND LEMON ZEST

DIFFICULTY LEVEL: ★☆☆ (EASY) | PREP: 5 MIN | COOK: 6 MIN | SERVES: 1

Ingredients

- 100g (3.5 oz) seedless red grapes, halved
- 40g (1.4 oz) whole milk ricotta
- 1/2 tsp lemon zest (1g)
- 1/2 tsp honey (3g)

Instructions:

1. In a small pan, simmer grapes over low heat for 5–6 minutes until softened into a compote.
2. Serve warm or chilled over ricotta. Top with lemon zest and honey.

Nutritional Facts (Per Serving): Calories: 199 | Carbs: 22g | Protein: 6g | Fat: 9g | Fiber: 2g | Sodium: 60mg | Sugars: 17g

CHAPTER 14: SNACK: Satisfying Mediterranean

SPICED LENTIL-APPLE BITES WITH YOGURT DIP

Nutritional Facts (Per Serving): Calories: 198 | Carbs: 22g | Protein: 9g | Fat: 7g | Fiber: 5g | Sodium: 260mg | Sugars: 6g

DIFFICULTY LEVEL: ★★☆ (MODERATE) | PREP: 10 MIN | COOK: 20 MIN | SERVES: 1

Ingredients

- For the bites:
- 50g cooked red lentils
- 40g grated apple (half a small apple)
- 1 tbsp rolled oats (10g)
- 1 egg white (33g)
- 1 tsp finely chopped parsley (1g)
- 1/4 tsp ground cumin (0.5g)
- Pinch of salt (0.25g)
- 1/2 tsp olive oil (2.5ml) – for baking tray
- For the dip:
- 2 tbsp plain Greek yogurt (40g)
- 1/4 tsp garlic powder (0.5g)
- 1/4 tsp lemon juice (1ml)

Instructions:

1. Preheat oven to 190°C (375°F).
2. In a bowl, mix lentils, grated apple, oats, egg white, parsley, cumin, and salt until combined.
3. Form 4 small round bites and place on an oiled baking sheet.
4. Bake for 18–20 minutes until firm and lightly golden.
5. In a small bowl, combine yogurt, garlic powder, and lemon juice. Serve warm lentil-apple bites with yogurt dip on the side.

MINI STUFFED PEPPERS WITH HERBED FETA AND OLIVES

Nutritional Facts (Per Serving): Calories: 194 | Carbs: 8g | Protein: 7g | Fat: 15g | Fiber: 2g | Sodium: 400mg | Sugars: 4g

DIFFICULTY LEVEL: ★☆☆ (EASY) | PREP: 8 MIN | COOK: 12 MIN | SERVES: 1

Ingredients

- 3 mini sweet bell peppers (120g)
- 30g (1 oz) feta cheese, crumbled
- 2 black olives, finely chopped (10g)
- 1 small tomato, diced (50g)
- 1/2 tsp dried oregano (0.5g)
- 1/2 tsp olive oil (2.5ml)
- 1/4 tsp lemon zest (0.5g)

Instructions:

1. Preheat oven to 200°C (400°F).
2. Slice off tops of peppers and remove seeds.
3. In a bowl, mix feta, tomato, olives, oregano, and lemon zest.
4. Stuff each pepper with the mixture and place on a baking tray.
5. Drizzle with olive oil and bake for 10–12 minutes until softened.
6. Serve warm or at room temperature.

ROASTED GRAPES WITH GOAT CHEESE AND WALNUTS

Nutritional Facts (Per Serving): Calories: 195 | Carbs: 19g | Protein: 5g | Fat: 12g | Fiber: 2g | Sodium: 100mg | Sugars: 15g

DIFFICULTY LEVEL: ★☆☆ (EASY) | PREP: 5 MIN | COOK: 10 MIN | SERVES: 1

Ingredients

- 80g seedless red grapes
- 20g soft goat cheese
- 5g chopped walnuts (about 1/2 tbsp)
- 1/4 tsp fresh rosemary, finely chopped (0.25g)
- 1/4 tsp olive oil (1.25ml)

Instructions:

1. Preheat oven to 200°C (400°F).
2. Place grapes on a baking tray, drizzle with olive oil and sprinkle with rosemary.
3. Roast for 10 minutes until grapes are soft and slightly blistered.
4. Spread goat cheese onto a small serving plate.
5. Top with roasted grapes and sprinkle with chopped walnuts.
6. Serve warm or room temperature.

CUCUMBER BOATS WITH TUNA, CAPERS & SUN-DRIED TOMATO

Nutritional Facts (Per Serving): Calories: 189 | Carbs: 6g | Protein: 17g | Fat: 11g | Fiber: 1g | Sodium: 380mg | Sugars: 3g

DIFFICULTY LEVEL: ★☆☆ (EASY) | PREP: 10 MIN | COOK: — | SERVES: 1

Ingredients

- 1 medium cucumber (150g)
- 60g canned tuna in water, drained
- 1 tbsp plain Greek yogurt (20g)
- 1 tsp chopped sun-dried tomatoes (5g)
- 1/2 tsp capers (2g)
- 1/4 tsp dried dill (0.5g)
- 1/4 tsp lemon juice (1ml)

Instructions:

1. Slice cucumber in half lengthwise and scoop out seeds to create boats.
2. In a bowl, combine tuna, yogurt, sun-dried tomatoes, capers, dill, and lemon juice.
3. Fill each cucumber half with the tuna mixture.
4. Serve chilled or at room temperature.

WARM DATE-ALMOND COUSCOUS CUPS

Nutritional Facts (Per Serving): Calories: 198 | Carbs: 29g | Protein: 5g | Fat: 7g | Fiber: 3g | Sodium: 55mg | Sugars: 13g

DIFFICULTY LEVEL: ★★☆ (MODERATE) | PREP: 10 MIN | COOK: 10 MIN | SERVES: 1

Ingredients

- 40g cooked couscous
- 3 dates, chopped (24g)
- 1 tbsp chopped almonds (10g)
- 1/2 tsp orange zest (1g)
- 1/2 tsp honey or maple syrup (3g)
- 1/8 tsp cinnamon (0.25g)
- 1/4 tsp olive oil (1.25ml)

Instructions:

1. Cook couscous if not already prepared.
2. In a small pan, lightly toast almonds for 2–3 minutes until golden.
3. In a bowl, mix couscous, chopped dates, almonds, orange zest, cinnamon, honey, and olive oil.
4. Press the warm mixture into two silicone muffin cups or ramekins.
5. Let rest 2–3 minutes to firm slightly and serve warm.

EGGPLANT CHIPS WITH TOMATO-FETA SALSA

Nutritional Facts (Per Serving): Calories: 193 | Carbs: 10g | Protein: 6g | Fat: 14g | Fiber: 4g | Sodium: 340mg | Sugars: 5g

DIFFICULTY LEVEL: ★★☆ (MODERATE) | PREP: 10 MIN | COOK: 15 MIN | SERVES: 1

Ingredients

- 80g eggplant, thinly sliced
- 1/2 tbsp olive oil (7ml)
- 50g fresh tomato, finely diced
- 20g feta cheese, crumbled
- 1/2 small garlic clove, minced (1g)
- 1 tsp chopped parsley (1g)
- 1/8 tsp black pepper (0.25g)

Instructions:

1. Preheat oven to 200°C (400°F).
2. Brush eggplant slices with olive oil and arrange on a baking sheet.
3. Bake for 12–15 minutes, flipping once, until crisp and golden.
4. In a bowl, combine tomato, feta, garlic, parsley, and pepper to form a salsa.
5. Serve the warm eggplant chips with the fresh tomato-feta salsa on top or on the side.

CHAPTER 15: DINNER: Vegetable-Focused & Light

SWEET POTATO & SPINACH STEW WITH PAPRIKA OIL

DIFFICULTY LEVEL: ★☆☆ (EASY) | PREP: 10 MIN | COOK: 20 MIN | SERVES: 1

Ingredients

- 100g sweet potato, diced
- 60g fresh spinach, chopped
- 1/2 onion, diced (40g)
- 1 tbsp olive oil (15ml)
- 1 garlic clove, minced (5g)
- 1/4 tsp smoked paprika (0.5g)
- 1/4 tsp cumin (0.5g)
- 300ml water or low-sodium vegetable broth
- 1/4 tsp salt (1g)
- Pinch pepper (0.25g)

Instructions:

1. Heat 1/2 tbsp olive oil in pot. Sauté onion and garlic 3 minutes.
2. Add sweet potato, cumin, salt, pepper. Stir and cook 2 minutes.
3. Pour in water, cover, simmer 10–12 minutes.
4. Add spinach, cook uncovered 3–5 minutes.
5. In small pan, heat remaining 1/2 tbsp olive oil with smoked paprika.
6. Drizzle paprika oil over stew before serving.

Nutritional Facts (Per Serving): Calories: 457 | Carbs: 49g | Protein: 10g | Fat: 25g | Fiber: 11g | Sodium: 345mg | Sugars: 9g

WHITE BEAN & SWISS CHARD SAUTÉ WITH LEMON AND OLIVE OIL

DIFFICULTY LEVEL: ★☆☆ (EASY) | PREP: 10 MIN | COOK: 15 MIN | SERVES: 1

Ingredients

- 120g cooked white beans
- 80g Swiss chard, chopped
- 1 tbsp olive oil (15ml)
- 1 small garlic clove, minced (5g)
- 1/2 lemon, juiced (15ml)
- 1/4 small onion, finely diced (20g)
- Pinch red pepper flakes (0.1g)
- 1/4 tsp salt (1g)
- Pinch black pepper (0.25g)

Instructions:

1. Heat olive oil in pan over medium. Add onion and garlic, cook 2–3 minutes.
2. Add Swiss chard, cook until wilted, 3–4 minutes.
3. Stir in white beans, salt, pepper, and red pepper flakes.
4. Cook together 3–4 minutes, then add lemon juice.
5. Stir well and serve warm.

Nutritional Facts (Per Serving): Calories: 495 | Carbs: 46g | Protein: 13g | Fat: 28g | Fiber: 10g | Sodium: 375mg | Sugars: 5g

BRAISED EGGPLANT WITH TOMATOES AND GARLIC

Nutritional Facts (Per Serving): Calories: 482 | Carbs: 43g | Protein: 9g | Fat: 30g | Fiber: 12g | Sodium: 390mg | Sugars: 11g

DIFFICULTY LEVEL: ★★☆ (MODERATE) | PREP: 10 MIN | COOK: 25 MIN | SERVES: 1

Ingredients

- 1 medium eggplant (250g), cubed
- 1 tbsp olive oil (15ml)
- 1 small onion, diced (50g)
- 2 garlic cloves, minced (10g)
- 1 medium tomato, chopped (100g)
- 1 tbsp tomato paste (15g)
- 1/4 tsp salt (1g)
- 1/4 tsp smoked paprika (0.5g)
- 1 tbsp chopped parsley (3g)
- Pinch black pepper (0.25g)

Instructions:

1. Heat olive oil in a skillet over medium heat.
2. Add onion and garlic, cook for 3 minutes until fragrant
3. Add cubed eggplant, cook 5 minutes, stirring often.
4. Add tomato, tomato paste, paprika, salt, pepper. Stir well. Cover and simmer for 15 minutes, stirring occasionally, until eggplant is tender.
5. Serve warm, garnished with parsley.

STUFFED ZUCCHINI WITH HERBED BULGUR AND TOMATOES

Nutritional Facts (Per Serving): Calories: 468 | Carbs: 55g | Protein: 11g | Fat: 23g | Fiber: 10g | Sodium: 360mg | Sugars: 10g

DIFFICULTY LEVEL: ★★☆ (MODERATE) | PREP: 15 MIN | COOK: 25 MIN | SERVES: 1

Ingredients

- 2 medium zucchini (300g)
- 40g dry bulgur
- 100ml water
- 1 medium tomato, diced (100g)
- 2 tbsp chopped onion (30g)
- 1 tbsp chopped fresh parsley (3g)
- 1/2 tbsp chopped fresh mint
- 1/2 tbsp olive oil (7ml)
- 1/2 tsp tomato paste (3g)
- 1 tbsp crumbled feta cheese (15g)
- 1/4 tsp salt (1g)
- Pinch black pepper (0.25g)
- Pinch dried oregano (0.25g)

Instructions:

1. Preheat oven to 200°C (400°F).
2. Cut zucchini in half lengthwise and scoop out centers to form boats. Reserve flesh.
3. Cook bulgur in 100ml boiling water until soft, about 10 minutes.
4. In a skillet, heat olive oil and sauté onion, reserved zucchini flesh, and tomato paste for 3–4 minutes.
5. Add diced tomato, bulgur, parsley, mint, salt, pepper, and oregano. Mix well and cook 2 more minutes.
6. Fill zucchini boats with the mixture. Top with crumbled feta.
7. Bake for 20–25 minutes until zucchini is tender and feta is lightly golden. Serve warm.

CAULIFLOWER BAKE WITH TOMATO, FETA, AND OREGANO

Nutritional Facts (Per Serving): Calories: 474 | Carbs: 28g | Protein: 17g | Fat: 32g | Fiber: 8g | Sodium: 460mg | Sugars: 10g

DIFFICULTY LEVEL: ★★☆ (MODERATE) | PREP: 10 MIN | COOK: 30 MIN | SERVES: 1

Ingredients

- 300g cauliflower florets
- 1 medium tomato, diced (100g)
- 30g crumbled feta cheese
- 1 small red onion, sliced (50g)
- 1 tbsp olive oil (15ml)
- 1 tsp dried oregano (1g)
- 1 egg (50g)
- 30ml milk or plant-based milk
- 1/4 tsp salt (1g)
- Pinch black pepper (0.25g)

Instructions:

1. Preheat oven to 200°C (400°F). Lightly grease small baking dish.
2. Steam cauliflower for 6–7 minutes until just tender. Drain and let cool slightly.
3. In a bowl, whisk egg, milk, oregano, salt, and pepper.
4. Layer steamed cauliflower, onion, and diced tomato in baking dish.
5. Pour egg mixture over vegetables. Top with crumbled feta and drizzle with olive oil.
6. Bake uncovered for 25–30 minutes until golden and set. Serve hot or warm.

CHICKPEA TAGINE WITH ROASTED CARROTS AND MINT

Nutritional Facts (Per Serving): Calories: 485 | Carbs: 52g | Protein: 15g | Fat: 24g | Fiber: 11g | Sodium: 410mg | Sugars: 13g

DIFFICULTY LEVEL: ★★☆ (MODERATE) | PREP: 10 MIN | COOK: 30 MIN | SERVES: 1

Ingredients

- 120g cooked chickpeas
- 2 medium carrots, cut into sticks (160g)
- 1 small onion, chopped (50g)
- 1 garlic clove, minced (5g)
- 1 tbsp olive oil (15ml)
- 1 tsp ground cumin (2g)
- 1/2 tsp ground cinnamon (1g)
- 1/2 tsp ground coriander (1g)
- 1 tbsp tomato paste (15g)
- 150ml water or light vegetable broth
- 1 tbsp chopped fresh mint
- 1/4 tsp salt (1g)
- Pinch black pepper (0.25g)

Instructions:

1. Preheat oven to 200°C (400°F). Roast carrots on tray with 1/2 tbsp olive oil, salt, and pepper for 20–25 minutes until golden. Meanwhile, in a skillet, heat remaining oil and sauté onion and garlic for 3 minutes.
2. Add cumin, cinnamon, coriander, and tomato paste. Stir well. Add chickpeas and water. Simmer gently for 10–12 minutes.
3. Stir in fresh mint and roasted carrots.
4. Serve warm as a rustic stew or over couscous if desired (not included in calories).

GRILLED VEGETABLES WITH LABNEH AND WALNUTS

Nutritional Facts (Per Serving): Calories: 492 | Carbs: 26g | Protein: 13g | Fat: 37g | Fiber: 8g | Sodium: 390mg | Sugars: 10g

DIFFICULTY LEVEL: ★☆☆ (EASY) | PREP: 10 MIN | COOK: 15 MIN | SERVES: 1

Ingredients

- 1/2 zucchini, sliced (100g)
- 1/2 red bell pepper, sliced (75g)
- 1/2 small eggplant, sliced (125g)
- 1 tbsp olive oil (15ml)
- 1/4 tsp salt (1g)
- Pinch black pepper (0.25g)
- 60g labneh or thick Greek yogurt
- 10g chopped walnuts 1 tbsp
- 1/2 garlic clove, finely grated (2g)
- 1 tsp lemon juice (5ml)
- 1 tbsp chopped parsley (3g)

Instructions:

1. Brush vegetables with olive oil and season with salt and pepper.
2. Grill or roast vegetables at 200°C (400°F) for 15 minutes, flipping once.
3. In a bowl, mix labneh with grated garlic and lemon juice.
4. Place grilled vegetables on a plate, spoon labneh over the top.
5. Sprinkle with chopped walnuts and parsley before serving.

POLENTA WITH ROASTED CHERRY TOMATOES AND THYME

Nutritional Facts (Per Serving): Calories: 478 | Carbs: 48g | Protein: 10g | Fat: 26g | Fiber: 5g | Sodium: 420mg | Sugars: 6g

DIFFICULTY LEVEL: ★☆☆ (EASY) | PREP: 10 MIN | COOK: 20 MIN | SERVES: 1

Ingredients

- 40g dry instant polenta
- 250ml water or low-sodium vegetable broth
- 100g cherry tomatoes
- 1 tbsp olive oil (15ml)
- 1 tsp fresh thyme leaves (1g)
- 1/2 tbsp grated Parmesan (5g)
- 1 tsp butter (5g)
- 1/4 tsp salt (1g)
- Pinch black pepper (0.25g)

Instructions:

1. Preheat oven to 200°C (400°F). Toss cherry tomatoes with 1/2 tbsp olive oil, thyme, salt, and pepper. Roast for 15–20 minutes until blistered.
2. In a small pot, bring water or broth to a boil. Slowly whisk in polenta.
3. Cook for 3–4 minutes over low heat, stirring constantly, until creamy.
4. Stir in butter and grated Parmesan. Season with a pinch of salt if needed.
5. Serve polenta in a shallow bowl, topped with roasted tomatoes and drizzle remaining 1/2 tbsp olive oil.

CHAPTER 16: DINNER: Seafood & Satisfaction

GRILLED SARDINES WITH LEMON AND PARSLEY OVER GREENS

DIFFICULTY LEVEL: ★★☆ (MODERATE) | **PREP:** 10 MIN | **COOK:** 10 MIN | **SERVES:** 1

Ingredients

- 3 whole fresh sardines (300g), cleaned
- 1 tbsp olive oil (15ml)
- 1 tbsp fresh lemon juice (15ml)
- 1 garlic clove, minced (5g)
- 1 tbsp chopped parsley (3g)
- 1 cup mixed greens (30g)
- 1/4 tsp salt (1g)
- Pinch black pepper (0.25g)

Instructions:

1. Rub sardines with olive oil, lemon juice, garlic, salt, and pepper.
2. Grill on high heat or broil 3–4 minutes per side until skin is crispy.
3. Serve over a bed of fresh greens, sprinkled with chopped parsley and extra lemon if desired.

Nutritional Facts (Per Serving): Calories: 486 | Carbs: 6g | Protein: 29g | Fat: 37g | Fiber: 2g | Sodium: 410mg | Sugars: 2g

BAKED COD WITH GARLIC CHICKPEAS AND SPINACH

DIFFICULTY LEVEL: ★★☆ (MODERATE) | **PREP:** 10 MIN | **COOK:** 20 MIN | **SERVES:** 1

Ingredients

- 150g cod fillet
- 100g cooked chickpeas
- 60g fresh spinach
- 1 garlic clove, minced (5g)
- 1/2 tbsp lemon juice (8ml)
- 1 tbsp olive oil (15ml)
- 1/4 tsp salt (1g)
- Pinch black pepper (0.25g)

Instructions:

1. Preheat oven to 200°C (400°F).
2. Place cod in a baking dish, season with salt, pepper, and lemon juice.
3. Bake for 12–15 minutes until flaky.
4. While cod bakes, heat olive oil in a pan. Add garlic, chickpeas, and spinach. Sauté 4–5 minutes.
5. Serve cod over the garlicky chickpea-spinach mixture.

Nutritional Facts (Per Serving): Calories: 495 | Carbs: 28g | Protein: 35g | Fat: 28g | Fiber: 7g | Sodium: 430mg | Sugars: 4g

SHRIMP & TOMATO SKILLET WITH CAPERS AND ZUCCHINI

DIFFICULTY LEVEL: ★☆☆ (EASY) | PREP: 10 MIN | COOK: 10 MIN | SERVES: 1

Ingredients

- 120g shrimp, peeled
- 1/2 zucchini, sliced (100g)
- 1 tomato, chopped (100g)
- 1 garlic clove, minced (5g)
- 1 tbsp olive oil (15ml)
- 1 tsp capers (5g)
- 1/4 tsp salt (1g)
- Pinch chili flakes (optional)
- Pinch black pepper (0.25g)
- 1 tbsp parsley, chopped (3g)

Instructions:

1. Heat olive oil in a skillet. Add garlic and zucchini. Sauté 3–4 minutes.
2. Add tomato, capers, salt, pepper, and chili flakes. Cook 2 minutes.
3. Add shrimp and cook until pink, about 3–4 minutes.
4. Serve hot, garnished with parsley.

Nutritional Facts (Per Serving): Calories: 472 | Carbs: 14g | Protein: 31g | Fat: 32g | Fiber: 4g | Sodium: 440mg | Sugars: 6g

TROUT FILLET WITH COUSCOUS AND ROASTED PEPPERS

DIFFICULTY LEVEL: ★★☆ (MODERATE) | PREP: 10 MIN | COOK: 20 MIN | SERVES: 1

Ingredients

- 140g trout fillet
- 1/4 cup dry couscous (45g)
- 1/2 red bell pepper, sliced (75g)
- 1 tsp lemon juice (5ml)
- 1 tbsp olive oil (15ml)
- 1/2 tsp dried oregano (1g)
- 1/4 tsp salt (1g)
- Pinch black pepper (0.25g)

Instructions:

1. Cook couscous with 100ml boiling water. Cover and let stand 5 minutes, then fluff.
2. Roast red pepper at 200°C (400°F) for 15–20 minutes until soft and charred.
3. Season trout with salt, pepper, oregano, and lemon.
4. Pan-fry trout in olive oil 3–4 minutes per side.
5. Serve fish over couscous with roasted pepper.

Nutritional Facts (Per Serving): Calories: 498 | Carbs: 31g | Protein: 30g | Fat: 30g | Fiber: 5g | Sodium: 420mg | Sugars: 6g

MACKEREL WITH WARM LENTIL SALAD AND RED ONION

Nutritional Facts (Per Serving): Calories: 489 | Carbs: 23g | Protein: 32g | Fat: 31g | Fiber: 7g | Sodium: 430mg | Sugars: 5g

DIFFICULTY LEVEL: ★★☆ (MODERATE) | PREP: 10 MIN | COOK: 20 MIN | SERVES: 1

Ingredients

- 100g cooked mackerel fillet
- 80g cooked green lentils
- 1/4 red onion, thinly sliced (30g)
- 1 tbsp olive oil (15ml)
- 1/2 tsp Dijon mustard (2g)
- 1 tsp red wine vinegar (5ml)
- 1 tbsp chopped parsley (3g)
- 1/4 tsp salt (1g)
- Pinch black pepper (0.25g)

Instructions:

1. Heat olive oil in a skillet. Lightly sauté red onion for 2–3 minutes until softened.
2. Add cooked lentils, salt, pepper, mustard, and vinegar. Stir and warm through for 3–4 minutes.
3. Place lentil salad on a plate. Top with mackerel fillet and fresh parsley.
4. Serve warm.

SEAFOOD & FENNEL SOUP WITH OLIVE DRIZZLE

Nutritional Facts (Per Serving): Calories: 472 | Carbs: 19g | Protein: 35g | Fat: 28g | Fiber: 4g | Sodium: 440mg | Sugars: 7g

DIFFICULTY LEVEL: ★★☆ (MODERATE) | PREP: 10 MIN | COOK: 25 MIN | SERVES: 1

Ingredients

- 80g shrimp, peeled
- 60g white fish (e.g., cod), cubed
- 1/4 fennel bulb, sliced (50g)
- 1/2 small potato, cubed (60g)
- 1 small tomato, chopped (80g)
- 1 garlic clove, minced (5g)
- 1 tbsp olive oil (15ml)
- 1/2 tsp dried oregano (1g)
- 1 cup water or seafood broth (240ml)
- 1/2 tbsp olive tapenade or finely chopped olives (10g)
- 1/4 tsp salt (1g)
- Pinch pepper (0.25g)

Instructions:

1. In a pot, heat 1/2 tbsp olive oil and sauté garlic and fennel for 3–4 minutes.
2. Add chopped tomato and potato, cook for 5 minutes.
3. Pour in water or broth, bring to a boil, reduce heat and simmer 10 minutes.
4. Add shrimp and fish, cook 5–6 minutes until seafood is opaque.
5. Serve with olive tapenade or olive oil drizzle on top.

CHAPTER 17: DINNER: Light Poultry Dishes

BRAISED CHICKEN THIGH WITH OLIVES AND TOMATOES

DIFFICULTY LEVEL: ★★☆ (MODERATE) | PREP: 10 MIN | COOK: 25 MIN | SERVES: 1

Ingredients

- 1 chicken thigh, skin-on, bone-in (160g)
- 1/2 cup cherry tomatoes, halved (80g)
- 6 black olives, pitted and sliced (20g)
- 1/2 small onion, sliced (40g)
- 1 garlic clove, minced (5g)
- 1 tbsp olive oil (15ml)
- 1/4 tsp dried thyme (0.5g)
- 1/4 tsp salt (1g)
- Pinch black pepper (0.25g)
- 1 tbsp chopped parsley (3g)

Instructions:

1. Season chicken thigh with salt, pepper, and thyme.
2. Heat olive oil in a skillet and brown chicken skin-side down for 5–6 minutes. Flip and cook another 3 minutes.
3. Add onion, garlic, tomatoes, and olives to the pan. Cover and simmer on low for 15 minutes.
4. Garnish with parsley and serve warm.

Nutritional Facts (Per Serving): Calories: 478 | Carbs: 12g | Protein: 32g | Fat: 32g | Fiber: 3g | Sodium: 470mg | Sugars: 6g

HERBED TURKEY MEATBALLS WITH SPINACH BULGUR PILAF

DIFFICULTY LEVEL: ★★☆ (MODERATE) | PREP: 15 MIN | COOK: 20 MIN | SERVES: 1

Ingredients

- 120g ground turkey
- 1 tbsp chopped parsley (3g)
- 1 tbsp chopped onion (10g)
- 1/4 tsp garlic powder (0.5g)
- 1/4 tsp salt (1g)
- Pinch pepper (0.25g)
- 1 tbsp olive oil (15ml)
- For the bulgur:
- 1/4 cup dry bulgur (45g)
- 1 cup spinach, chopped (30g)
- 1/2 tsp lemon juice (2.5ml)
- 1 tsp olive oil (5ml)

Instructions:

1. Mix turkey with onion, parsley, garlic powder, salt, and pepper. Form small meatballs.
2. Heat 1 tbsp olive oil in a pan and cook meatballs for 8–10 minutes until browned and cooked through.
3. Cook bulgur in 100ml water until tender, fluff with fork.
4. Stir in spinach, lemon juice, and 1 tsp olive oil. Serve meatballs over bulgur.

Nutritional Facts (Per Serving): Calories: 499 | Carbs: 28g | Protein: 36g | Fat: 28g | Fiber: 5g | Sodium: 460mg | Sugars: 4g

CHICKEN WITH ROASTED EGGPLANT AND GARLIC YOGURT

Nutritional Facts (Per Serving): Calories: 480 | Carbs: 15g | Protein: 35g | Fat: 31g | Fiber: 5g | Sodium: 440mg | Sugars: 6g

DIFFICULTY LEVEL: ★★☆ (MODERATE) | **PREP:** 10 MIN | **COOK:** 25 MIN | **SERVES:** 1

Ingredients

- 1 chicken breast (150g)
- 1/2 medium eggplant, cubed (100g)
- 1 tbsp olive oil (15ml)
- 1 garlic clove, minced (5g)
- 1/3 cup plain Greek yogurt (80g)
- 1/2 tsp lemon juice (2.5ml)
- 1/4 tsp salt (1g)
- Pinch cumin (0.2g)
- Pinch black pepper (0.25g)
- 1 tbsp chopped mint or parsley (3g)

Instructions:

1. Roast cubed eggplant at 200°C (400°F) for 20 minutes until golden.
2. Season chicken and pan-cook with 1/2 tbsp oil for 6–7 minutes per side until cooked through.
3. Mix yogurt with garlic, lemon, cumin, salt, and pepper.
4. Serve chicken with roasted eggplant and garlic yogurt sauce. Garnish with herbs.

LEMON CHICKEN SKILLET WITH ZUCCHINI AND PEPPERS

Nutritional Facts (Per Serving): Calories: 488 | Carbs: 18g | Protein: 33g | Fat: 31g | Fiber: 5g | Sodium: 435mg | Sugars: 7g

DIFFICULTY LEVEL: ★★☆ (MODERATE) | **PREP:** 10 MIN | **COOK:** 20 MIN | **SERVES:** 1

Ingredients

- 1 chicken breast (150g)
- 1/2 zucchini, sliced (100g)
- 1/2 bell pepper, sliced (75g)
- 1 garlic clove, minced (5g)
- 1 tbsp olive oil (15ml)
- 1/2 tbsp lemon juice (7ml)
- 1/4 tsp oregano (0.5g)
- 1/4 tsp salt (1g)
- Pinch black pepper (0.25g)
- 1 tbsp chopped parsley (3g)

Instructions:

1. Season chicken with salt, pepper, and oregano.
2. Sear chicken in olive oil for 6–7 minutes per side until golden and cooked through. Remove and keep warm.
3. Sauté zucchini, pepper, and garlic in the same skillet for 5–6 minutes.
4. Add lemon juice, stir, and return chicken to skillet. Cook 2 more minutes.
5. Serve hot, topped with parsley.

STUFFED PEPPERS WITH GROUND TURKEY AND COUSCOUS

Nutritional Facts (Per Serving): Calories: 492 | Carbs: 29g | Protein: 35g | Fat: 26g | Fiber: 5g | Sodium: 440mg | Sugars: 6g

DIFFICULTY LEVEL: ★★☆ (MODERATE) | PREP: 10 MIN | COOK: 25 MIN | SERVES: 1

Ingredients

- 1 medium bell pepper (150g)
- 100g ground turkey
- 1/4 cup dry couscous (45g)
- 1 tbsp olive oil (15ml)
- 1/4 small onion, finely chopped (20g)
- 1 garlic clove, minced (5g)
- 1 tbsp chopped parsley (3g)
- 1/4 tsp paprika (0.5g)
- 1/4 tsp salt (1g)
- Pinch black pepper (0.25g)

Instructions:

1. Preheat oven to 200°C (400°F). Cut top off pepper and remove seeds.
2. Cook couscous with 60ml boiling water and fluff with a fork.
3. Sauté onion and garlic in olive oil for 2 minutes, then add ground turkey and cook until no longer pink.
4. Mix turkey with couscous, parsley, paprika, salt, and pepper.
5. Stuff the pepper with the mixture and bake for 15–18 minutes. Serve hot.

POACHED CHICKEN WITH LENTILS AND LEMON-PARSLEY OIL

Nutritional Facts (Per Serving): Calories: 478 | Carbs: 22g | Protein: 36g | Fat: 28g | Fiber: 6g | Sodium: 420mg | Sugars: 3g

DIFFICULTY LEVEL: ★★☆ (MODERATE) | PREP: 10 MIN | COOK: 20 MIN | SERVES: 1

Ingredients

- 1 chicken breast (150g)
- 80g cooked lentils
- 1 bay leaf
- 1 garlic clove, crushed (5g)
- 1 tbsp chopped parsley (3g)
- 1 tbsp olive oil (15ml)
- 1/2 tbsp lemon juice (7ml)
- 1/4 tsp salt (1g)
- Pinch black pepper (0.25g)

Instructions:

1. Bring water to a simmer with bay leaf and garlic. Add chicken breast and poach for 12–15 minutes until cooked through.
2. Meanwhile, mix olive oil, parsley, lemon juice, salt, and pepper in a bowl.
3. Warm lentils in a small pan.
4. Serve chicken sliced over lentils and drizzle with lemon-parsley oil.

GRILLED CHICKEN WITH TOMATO, OLIVE, AND ARUGULA SALAD

DIFFICULTY LEVEL: ★☆☆ (EASY) | PREP: 10 MIN | COOK: 15 MIN | SERVES: 1

Ingredients

- 1 chicken breast (150g)
- 1 tbsp olive oil (15ml)
- 1/2 cup cherry tomatoes, halved (80g)
- 5 Kalamata olives, sliced (20g)
- 1 cup arugula (30g)
- 1/2 tbsp balsamic vinegar (7ml)
- 1/4 tsp dried oregano (0.5g)
- Salt and pepper to taste

Instructions:

1. Season chicken with oregano, salt, and pepper.
2. Grill for 6–7 minutes per side until fully cooked.
3. Toss tomatoes, olives, and arugula with olive oil and balsamic vinegar.
4. Slice chicken and serve over salad.

Nutritional Facts (Per Serving): Calories: 485 | Carbs: 14g | Protein: 37g | Fat: 32g | Fiber: 4g | Sodium: 450mg | Sugars: 5g

WARM CHICKPEA-CHICKEN BOWL WITH MINT YOGURT

DIFFICULTY LEVEL: ★★☆ (MODERATE) | PREP: 10 MIN | COOK: 20 MIN | SERVES: 1

Ingredients

- 100g cooked chicken breast, cubed
- 100g cooked chickpeas
- 1/4 zucchini, diced (50g)
- 1 tbsp olive oil (15ml)
- 1/3 cup plain Greek yogurt (80g)
- 1 tbsp chopped mint (3g)
- 1/2 tbsp lemon juice (7ml)
- 1/4 tsp cumin (0.5g)
- 1/4 tsp salt (1g)
- Pinch black pepper (0.25g)

Instructions:

1. Sauté zucchini and chickpeas in olive oil for minutes with cumin and salt.
2. Add cooked chicken, warm through for 2–3 minutes.
3. Mix yogurt with mint, lemon juice, salt, and pepper.
4. Serve chicken-chickpea bowl topped with mint yogurt.

Nutritional Facts (Per Serving): Calories: 490 | Carbs: 28g | Protein: 36g | Fat: 29g | Fiber: 7g | Sodium: 430mg | Sugars: 6g

CHAPTER 18: DINNER: Grain & Plant Harmony

FARRO SALAD WITH ROASTED VEGETABLES AND FETA

DIFFICULTY LEVEL: ★★☆ (MODERATE) | **PREP:** 10 MIN | **COOK:** 25 MIN | **SERVES:** 1

Ingredients

- 1/4 cup dry farro (45g)
- 1/2 small zucchini, chopped (75g)
- 1/2 red bell pepper, chopped (75g)
- 1/2 small red onion, chopped (40g)
- 1 tbsp olive oil (15ml)
- 25g feta cheese, crumbled
- 1 tsp lemon juice (5ml)
- 1/4 tsp oregano (0.5g)
- Salt and pepper to taste

Instructions:

1. Cook farro in boiling water until tender, about 20 minutes. Drain and cool.
2. Meanwhile, roast zucchini, bell pepper, and onion with olive oil, salt, and pepper at 200°C (400°F) for 20 minutes.
3. Combine farro with roasted vegetables, feta, lemon juice, and oregano. Toss gently and serve warm or room temperature.

Nutritional Facts (Per Serving): Calories: 494 | Carbs: 39g | Protein: 17g | Fat: 30g | Fiber: 7g | Sodium: 450mg | Sugars: 6g

WARM LENTILS WITH CARROTS, LEEKS, AND TAHINI DRIZZLE

DIFFICULTY LEVEL: ★★☆ (MODERATE) | **PREP:** 10 MIN | **COOK:** 20 MIN | **SERVES:** 1

Ingredients

- 80g cooked lentils
- 1/2 carrot, thinly sliced (50g)
- 1/2 leek, white part only, sliced (60g)
- 1 garlic clove, minced (5g)
- 1 tbsp olive oil (15ml)
- 1 tbsp tahini (15g)
- 1 tsp lemon juice (5ml)
- 1 tbsp water (15ml)
- 1/4 tsp salt (1g)
- Pinch of black pepper (0.25g)
- Fresh parsley to garnish

Instructions:

1. Sauté carrot, leek, and garlic in olive oil over medium heat for 6–7 minutes until soft.
2. Add lentils, season with salt and pepper, and cook for another 5 minutes.
3. In a bowl, whisk tahini with lemon juice, water, and a pinch of salt until smooth.
4. Serve lentil mixture warm, drizzled with tahini sauce and garnished with parsley.

Nutritional Facts (Per Serving): Calories: 488 | Carbs: 34g | Protein: 20g | Fat: 30g | Fiber: 9g | Sodium: 420mg | Sugars: 7g

BARLEY PILAF WITH MUSHROOMS AND CUMIN YOGURT

Nutritional Facts (Per Serving): Calories: 482 | Carbs: 36g | Protein: 18g | Fat: 29g | Fiber: 7g | Sodium: 440mg | Sugars: 5g

DIFFICULTY LEVEL: ★★☆ (MODERATE) | PREP: 10 MIN | COOK: 25 MIN | SERVES: 1

Ingredients

- 1/4 cup dry pearl barley (50g)
- 1/2 cup mushrooms, sliced (75g)
- 1 small shallot, chopped (30g)
- 1 tbsp olive oil (15ml)
- 1/3 cup plain Greek yogurt (80g)
- 1/4 tsp cumin (0.5g)
- 1/2 tsp lemon juice (2.5ml)
- Salt and pepper to taste
- Fresh parsley to garnish

Instructions:

1. Cook barley in boiling water until tender, about 25 minutes. Drain.
2. Sauté mushrooms and shallots in olive oil for 6–7 minutes until golden.
3. Mix yogurt with cumin, lemon juice, and a pinch of salt.
4. Toss cooked barley with sautéed mushrooms. Serve with cumin yogurt and parsley.

QUINOA BOWL WITH ZUCCHINI, CHICKPEAS, AND LEMON OIL

Nutritional Facts (Per Serving): Calories: 489 | Carbs: 38g | Protein: 19g | Fat: 28g | Fiber: 8g | Sodium: 410mg | Sugars: 5g

DIFFICULTY LEVEL: ★★☆ (MODERATE) | PREP: 10 MIN | COOK: 15 MIN | SERVES: 1

Ingredients

- 1/4 cup dry quinoa (45g)
- 1/2 small zucchini, diced (75g)
- 80g cooked chickpeas
- 1 tbsp olive oil (15ml)
- 1 tsp lemon zest (2g)
- 1/2 tbsp lemon juice (7ml)
- 1/4 tsp cumin (0.5g)
- Salt and pepper to taste
- Fresh parsley or mint to garnish

Instructions:

1. Cook quinoa in 100ml water until fluffy, about 12–15 minutes.
2. Sauté zucchini in 1/2 tbsp olive oil until lightly browned.
3. Toss cooked quinoa with chickpeas, zucchini, lemon zest, juice, cumin, and remaining oil.
4. Season to taste, garnish with herbs, and serve warm.

BROWN RICE WITH TOMATO, SPINACH, AND PINE NUTS

DIFFICULTY LEVEL: ★★★ (EASY) | PREP: 10 MIN | COOK: 20 MIN | SERVES: 1

Ingredients

- 1/4 cup dry brown rice (45g)
- 1/2 medium tomato, diced (60g)
- 1 cup fresh spinach, chopped (30g)
- 1 tbsp olive oil (15ml)
- 1 tbsp pine nuts (10g)
- 1 garlic clove, minced (5g)
- Salt and pepper to taste

Instructions:

1. Cook brown rice in water until tender, about 20 minutes. Drain if needed.
2. Heat olive oil in a pan. Add garlic and tomato, cook for 3 minutes.
3. Add spinach and cook until wilted.
4. Stir in cooked rice and season with salt and pepper.
5. Top with toasted pine nuts and serve warm.

Nutritional Facts (Per Serving): Calories: 491 | Carbs: 41g | Protein: 13g | Fat: 30g | Fiber: 5g | Sodium: 390mg | Sugars: 4g

MILLET WITH ROASTED CAULIFLOWER AND RAISINS

DIFFICULTY LEVEL: ★★☆ (MODERATE) | PREP: 10 MIN | COOK: 25 MIN | SERVES: 1

Ingredients

- 1/4 cup dry millet (45g)
- 1 cup cauliflower florets (120g)
- 1 tbsp olive oil (15ml)
- 1 tbsp raisins (15g)
- 1/2 tsp ground cumin (1g)
- 1/8 tsp cinnamon (0.3g)
- Salt and pepper to taste
- Fresh parsley to garnish

Instructions:

1. Cook millet in water until tender, about 15–20 minutes.
2. Roast cauliflower at 200°C (400°F) for 20 minutes with olive oil, cumin, salt, and pepper.
3. Stir raisins and cinnamon into millet during last 2 minutes of cooking.
4. Mix roasted cauliflower with millet. Garnish with parsley and serve.

Nutritional Facts (Per Serving): Calories: 489 | Carbs: 47g | Protein: 11g | Fat: 28g | Fiber: 6g | Sodium: 380mg | Sugars: 9g

COUSCOUS WITH ROASTED SQUASH, CHICKPEAS, AND HERBS

Nutritional Facts (Per Serving): Calories: 492 | Carbs: 46g | Protein: 14g | Fat: 29g | Fiber: 6g | Sodium: 400mg | Sugars: 6g

DIFFICULTY LEVEL: ★★☆ (MODERATE) | PREP: 10 MIN | COOK: 25 MIN | SERVES: 1

Ingredients

- 1/4 cup dry couscous (45g)
- 3/4 cup diced butternut squash (100g)
- 80g cooked chickpeas
- 1 tbsp olive oil (15ml)
- 1 tbsp chopped fresh parsley (3g)
- 1/4 tsp ground coriander (0.5g)
- Salt and pepper to taste
- Juice of 1/4 lemon (7ml)

Instructions:

1. Roast squash at 200°C (400°F) for 20 minutes with olive oil, salt, and coriander.
2. Cook couscous with 60ml boiling water, then fluff with a fork.
3. Mix couscous with chickpeas, roasted squash, parsley, and lemon juice.
4. Season to taste and serve warm or at room temperature.

WILD RICE & ROASTED EGGPLANT WITH GARLIC SAUCE

Nutritional Facts (Per Serving): Calories: 495 | Carbs: 40g | Protein: 12g | Fat: 32g | Fiber: 8g | Sodium: 410mg | Sugars: 6g

DIFFICULTY LEVEL: ★★☆ (MODERATE) | PREP: 10 MIN | COOK: 25 MIN | SERVES: 1

Ingredients

- 1/4 cup wild rice (45g)
- 1/2 medium eggplant, diced (100g)
- 1 tbsp olive oil (15ml)
- 1 garlic clove, minced (5g)
- 2 tbsp plain yogurt (40g)
- 1 tsp lemon juice (5ml)
- Salt and pepper to taste
- Fresh mint or parsley to garnish

Instructions:

1. Cook wild rice in water until tender, about 25 minutes.
2. Roast eggplant at 200°C (400°F) for 20 minutes with olive oil and salt.
3. Whisk yogurt with garlic, lemon juice, and a pinch of salt to make the sauce.
4. Serve eggplant over rice, topped with garlic sauce and fresh herbs.

APPENDIX MEASUREMENT CONVERSION CHART

VOLUME EQUIVALENTS (DRY)

US STANDARD	METRIC (APPROXIMATE)
1/8 teaspoon	0.5 mL
1/4 teaspoon	1 mL
1/2 teaspoon	2 mL
3/4 teaspoon	4 mL
1 teaspoon	5 mL
1 tablespoon	15 mL
1/4 cup	59 mL
1/2 cup	118 mL
3/4 cup	177 mL
1 cup	235 mL
2 cups	475 mL
3 cups	700 mL
4 cups	1 L

VOLUME EQUIVALENTS (LIQUID)

US STANDARD	US STANDARD (OUNCES)	METRIC (APPROXIMATE)
2 tablespoons	1 fl.oz.	30 mL
1/4 cup	2 fl.oz.	60 mL
1/2 cup	4 fl.oz.	120 mL
1 cup	8 fl.oz.	240 mL
1 1/2 cup	12 fl.oz.	355 mL
2 cups or 1 pint	16 fl.oz.	475 mL
4 cups or 1 quart	32 fl.oz.	1 L
1 gallon	128 fl.oz.	4 L

WEIGHT EQUIVALENTS

US STANDARD	METRIC (APPROXIMATE)
1 ounce	28 g
2 ounces	57 g
5 ounces	142 g
10 ounces	284 g
15 ounces	425 g
16 ounces (1 pound)	455 g
(1 pound)	680 g
1.5 pounds	907 g

TEMPERATURES EQUIVALENTS

FAHRENHEIT(F)	CELSIUS(C) (APPROXIMATE)
225 °F	107 °C
250 °F	120 °C
275 °F	135 °C
300 °F	150 °C
325 °F	160 °C
350 °F	180 °C
375 °F	190 °C
400 °F	205 °C
425 °F	220 °C
450 °F	235 °C
475 °F	245 °C
500 °F	260 °C

Printed in Dunstable, United Kingdom